ORIGINS

The term 'Battlecruiser' can be precisely defined for the period 1905-1920 as indicating a ship at least 4 knots faster than contemporary battleships, mounting a type of gun suitable for the main armament of the latter and with as much protection as could be worked in after other requirements had been met. The difficulty of producing a satisfactory design on a displacement which might be less than that of contemporary battleships, and with a few exceptions was never much greater, lay in the bulk and weight of the boilers and engines needed for the higher speed. In producing a tough and formidable fighting ship of this type, the Germans were more successful than the British during the period under review. Subsequently the magnificent British 'G 3' design, which the writer has already described in detail in *Warship* Numbers 1-4, was

cancelled under the Washington treaty of 1922, and by the 1930s machinery weights had fallen so much that it was possible to give battleships the speed of battlecruisers and the two types merged, though there was a difference of 6 knots between the fastest and the slowest.

The origins of the first battlecruisers, the British *Invincible* class laid down in 1906, go back 12 years to the large, and for their day fast, cruisers *Powerful* and *Terrible*. With an actual displacement of 14 345 tons they were nearly as large as the *Majestic* class battleships, could do 22 kts — over 4 kts more than the *Majestics* — with 25 000 ihp from 48 Belleville boilers and 2 sets of triple-expansion engines. Their principal armament of 2-9.2in and 12, later 16-6in guns was puny compared to the battleship's 4-12in and 12-6in, particularly as the 9.2in/40 cal had a rather lower muzzle velocity than the 12in/35.4 cal and their protection was despicable. There was no side armour and the thick plates of the armour deck slope usually given as 6in Harvey, were actually 4in mild steel. The shallow 2ft 8in deep 9.2in barbettes were armoured with 6in Harvey as

Indomitable leading *Inflexible* at full speed and cleared for action in the North Sea, 1918
By courtesy of John Roberts

were the shield faces, but the ammunition tubes which led to the armour deck, here only 2½in, were given nothing better than 3in mild steel. For comparison the *Majestic* had a 9in belt, 14—7in barbettes down to the armour deck and 10½in turret faces, all Harvey though the last item in some of the class was Nickel steel.

The next British cruisers of about this size the *Drake* class, were provided with side armour and details of them and their successors the *Duke of Edinburgh, Warrior* and *Minotaur* classes are given in Table 1. There is a very marked improvement in armament between the *Drake* and *Duke of Edinburgh* and again to a lesser extent between the latter and the *Warrior* with the removal of the main deck 6in guns, sited too near the waterline. From the point of gunpower the *Minotaur's* were the best, and they would have been better still if the idea of 4 high velocity 10in/50cal guns to surpass those in the US *Tennessee* class had been adopted instead of 9.2in at the price of perhaps 4—7.5in which would have eased the problem of the dangerous ammunition passages, which when action was thought probable, contained about half the 7.5in charges in thin, not flash-proof nor even air-tight, steel lockers.

TABLE 1	**COMPARISON OF BRITISH ARMOURED CRUISER CLASSES**			
Ships	**Drake**	**Duke of Edinburgh**	**Warrior**	**Minotaur**
LAID DOWN	1899	1903	1903-4	1905
COMPLETED	1902-3	1906	1907	1908-9
NORMAL DISPLACEMENT (TONS)	13 920	12 595	13 240	14 595
DEEP LOAD DISPLACEMENT (TONS)	15 445	14 050	14 440	16 085
LENGTH (PP/OA-FT)	500/533½	480/505½	480/505½	490/519
BEAM (FT IN)	71 0	73 6	73 6	74 6 (*Shannon* 75 6)
MEAN DRAUGHT (FT IN)	25 7½	25 6½	26 4¾	25 11½ (*Shannon* 25 0)
MAIN ARMAMENT (INCH)	2-9.2/46.7cal	6-9.2/46.7cal	6-9.2/46.7cal	4-9.2/50.1cal
SECONDARY ARMAMENT (INCH)	16-6/44.9cal	10-6/50cal	4-7.5/50cal	10-7.5/50cal
ANTI-TBD ARMAMENT (PDR)	14-12/12cwt	20-3 Vickers	24-3 Vickers	16-12/18 cwt
TORPEDO-TUBES (INCH)	2-18	3-18	3-18	5-18
ARMOUR (INCHES)				
BELT	6-2	6-3	6-3	6-3
UPPER BELT	Nil	6 battery	6	Nil
MAIN TURRETS	6 max	7½ max	7½ max	8 max
MAIN BARBETTES	6	6 max	6 max	7 max
SECONDARY GUNS	5 casemates	6 battery	8 max turrets 6 max barbettes	8 max turrets 7 max barbettes
TURRET CROWNS	2	2	2	9.2in-3, 7.5in-2
CONNING TOWER	12	10	10	10
DECK AT UPPER EDGE SIDE ARMOUR	1½	1-¾	1-¾	1½-1 local only
LOWER ARMOUR DECK	1, 2½ aft	¾, 2-1½ aft	¾, 2-1½ aft	2-1½, 2 fore & aft
IHP; SPEED (KNOTS)	30 000=23	23 500=23	23 500=22½- 23	27 000=23 (*Shannon* 22¼)
COAL, NORMAL/DEEP LOAD (TONS)	1250/2580	1000/2200	1000/2050	1000/2060 (*Shannon* 950/2020)
OIL FUEL (TONS)	Nil	600	600	750
BROADSIDE, MAIN & SECONDARY GUNS (LBS)	1560	2020	1920	2520
LESS MAIN DECK GUNS	1160	1520	1920	2520

Normal and deep load displacements are the average actual figures for the class. The deep load figures do not include oil fuel, and mean draught is for the normal displacement as above.

The above armour figures are flattering. The 6in belt only ran for 257ft in the *Drake*, 260ft in the next two classes and 272ft in the *Minotaur*, being 4in abeam of the fore barbette in all, and 3in abeam of the after one except in the *Drake's* where there was here no side armour. The fore and aft single 9.2in barbettes in the first three classes were shallow armour rings 4ft deep with 3in floors and 3in mild steel ammunition tubes to the main deck only, except for the after tube in *Drake* which ran to the lower deck. The wing 9.2in barbettes in *Duke of Edinburgh* and *Warrior* were reduced to 3in on their inboard sides with 1in floors and had no ammunition tubes, the 7.5in in *Warrior* being similar except that the barbette rings were only 2ft 10in deep. The twin 9.2in barbettes in *Minotaur* were deeper, the fore one having a 7in mild steel ammunition tube to the main deck and 3in to the lower deck, and the after one being taken down to the main deck with a 4in tube to the lower deck. The single 7.5in barbettes had 3in floors and ammunition tubes 7in to the main deck and 2in to the lower deck, but were still 2ft 10in deep.

It is hardly necessary to compare each class with its battleship contemporary but it may be noted that the *Agamemnon* laid down and completed 4 months after the *Minotaur* had 4—12in/45cal, 10—9.2in/50.1cal (broadside 5300lb), 12in maximum side armour, and could do 18—18½kts with about 17 000 ihp on an actual normal displacement of 15 925 tons.

The only German examples of this type of armoured cruiser were the famous *Scharnhorst* and *Gneisenau* as the *Fürst Bismarck* was at best a 19kt ship.

Their guns were not powerful, the 8.3in firing a 238lb shell at 2550fs (80°F) so that the broadside was 1692lb from 8.3in and 5.9in, but the turrets allowed 30° elevation giving a range of 17 800 yards through the 8.3in battery guns were limited to 16° and 13 600 yards. For comparison the *Minotaur's* 9.2in Mk XI fired a 380lb shell at 2875fs and her 7.5in Mk V 200lb at 2830fs, but the 15° mountings limited ranges to 16 200 and 14 200 yards. It is hard to see any connection between the *Scharnhorst* and the subsequent German battlecruisers, or indeed any particular virtues in her design, and the undoubted fame of the two ships must be credited to the excellence of their gunnery officers and men.

Large armoured cruisers were built in the United States, France and Russia of which the most notable feature was perhaps the 4-10in/40cal guns of unusual power for their length — 510lb shell, 2700fs — mounted in the *Tennessee* class, laid down in 1903-5 and completed in 1906-8. The French armoured cruisers which had nothing heavier than 7.6in guns, will not be described nor will the earlier Russian, none of which could do more than 20kts. The *Rurik* was, however, a ship of considerable interest, and in some respects very advanced for her date (see Table 2).

TABLE 2 **COMPARISON OF FOREIGN ARMOURED CRUISERS**

Ship or class	Scharnhorst	Tennessee	Rurik	Blücher
LAID DOWN	1904-5	1903-5	1905	1907
COMPLETED	1907-8	1906-8	1908	1910
NORMAL DISPLACEMENT (TONS)	11 433	14 500	15 170	15 590
DEEP LOAD DISPLACEMENT (TONS)	12 780	15 715/15 981	c.16 500	17 250
LENGTH (OA - FT)	474½	504½	529	530½
BEAM (FT IN)	70 10	72 11	75	80 3
MEAN DRAUGHT (FT IN)	24 7	25	26	26 3
MAIN ARMAMENT (INCH)	8-8.3/40	4-10/40	4-10/48.5	12-8.3/45
SECONDARY ARMAMENT (INCH)	6-5.9/40	16-6/50	8-8/48.5	8-5.9/45
ANTI-TBD ARMAMENT (INCH)	20-3.45/35	22-3/50	20-4.7/48.5	16-3.45/45
TORPEDO-TUBES (INCH)	4-18	4-21	2-18	4-18
ARMOUR (inches)				
BELT	6-3.2	5-3	6-3	7-2.4
UPPER BELT	6 battery	5-2 battery	3	5½ battery
MAIN TURRETS	6¾	9-5	8	7-5½
MAIN BARBETTES	6¾-5½	8-4	7¼-2	7
SECONDARY GUNS	6	5	7-1½	5½
TURRET CROWNS	1.2	2½	2½	3.2-2.4
CONNING TOWER	8	9	8	10
DECK AT UPPER EDGE SIDE ARMOUR	1-0.8	—	1½	—
LOWER ARMOUR DECK	2¼-1½	4-1½	1½-1	2.8-1.2
TORPEDO BULKHEAD	—	—	1½	1.2
IHP; SPEED (KNOTS)	26 000=22.5	27 500=22	19 700=21	34 000=24½
COAL: NORMAL/DEEP LOAD (TONS)	790/1970	900/1950	1200/2000	885/2260
OIL FUEL (TONS)	—	—	200	—
BROADSIDE, MAIN AND SECONDARY GUNS (LBS)	1692	2880	2976	2304
LESS MAIN DECK GUNS	1216	2250	2976	1904

INVINCIBLE CLASS
INVINCIBLE, INFLEXIBLE, INDOMITABLE

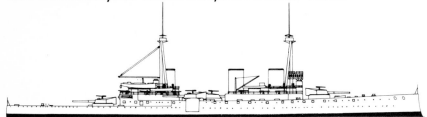

Invincible class, as designed, 1905

TABLE 3: **INVINCIBLE CLASS PARTICULARS**

Dimensions: 530ft (pp) 562½ft (wl) 567ft (oa) x 78ft 6in x 26ft 0in mean.
Legend displacement: 17 250tons
Actual normal displacement (with fore and aft draught): *Indomitable* 17 410 (25ft 6in/26ft 7in); *Inflexible* 17 290 (25ft 1in/26ft 8in); *Invincible* 17 330 (24ft 7in/27ft 0in).
Deep load (less oil fuel): Respectively 20 125, 19 975, 19 940 tons.
Sinkage: 69.8tons/inch, mean full load draught 29ft 9in.
Freeboard: 30ft forward, 22ft amidships, 17ft 2in aft.

	Builder	**Machinery**	**Laid down**	**Launched**	**Completed**
INDOMITABLE	Fairfield	Fairfield	1.3.1906	16.3.1907	.10.1908*
INFLEXIBLE	Clydebank	Clydebank	5.2.1906	26.6.1907	.10.1908
INVINCIBLE	Elswick	Humphreys, Tennant	2.4.1906	13.4.1907	.3.1909

Indomitable was commissioned for particular service, the Quebec Tercentenary celebration, 25 June 1908 but on her return to Chatham on 10 August was handed over to her contractors for completion at Chatham.

Invincible, 1910
By courtesy of John Roberts

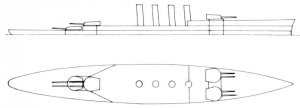

DESIGN 'A':
17 000 tons, 540ft (pp) x 77ft x 26½ft 8-12in/45, with gun axis heights of 34ft forward and 20ft and 12ft aft; 13-4in, 5 TT, 6in maximum side armour from 6ft 6in above to 4ft 6in below lwl, 8in maximum on 12in guns. Designed ihp 41 000=25½kts.

DESIGN 'B':
As 'A' except 17 200 tons, 6in more beam. Gun axis heights 34ft and 22ft.

DESIGN 'C':
15 600 tons, 520ft x 76ft x 26ft.

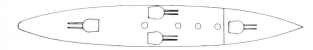

DESIGN 'D':
As 'A' except 17 750 tons, 550ft x 79ft x 26½ft. Gun axis heights 34ft, 30ft, 21ft.

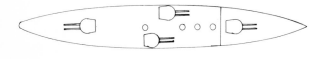

DESIGN 'E':
As 'D' except arrangement of turrets.

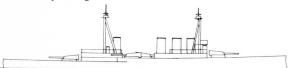

DESIGN

The original sketch designs considered by the 1905 Committee on Designs were all for 25kt ships with reciprocating engines. There was nothing impossible in this as the German *Blücher* did 25.86kts on the mile. The first design 'A' was prepared by Chief Constructor Gard for Admiral Sir John Fisher (see drawings). However, objections were made to the superfiring guns and to the cut-down hull aft, and Design 'B' prepared for the Committee by Constructor Narbeth: an alternative design 'C' had the forward guns sited with a longer forecastle ahead of them, and only a single twin turret aft giving 6—12in.

Design 'D' had a twin turret on the centreline forward and aft and 2 abreast in a common redoubt amidships which was modified in Design 'E' (otherwise similar) to an echelon arrangement so that firing was possible on the opposite beam through about 30° if the other turret was disabled. Armour was similar to that of the previous designs, the 4in guns were increased to 14 and ihp to 42 500. Over-optimistic estimates of the machinery weight savings from turbines were made, the most realistic assuming a saving of 12½% which modified Design 'E' to 540ft x 79ft x 26ft and 16 850 tons. This design became the basis of the first battlecruisers, though the 3 ships ordered under the 1905-6 programme differed in many ways.

ARMAMENT

The main armament of 8—12in/45cal Mark X guns was in 4 twin turrets, one forward and one aft and two slightly echelonned amidships, but with individual barbettes and not in a common redoubt. The gun axis heights were 'A' 32, 'P' and 'Q' 28, 'X' 21ft. At the battle of the Falkland Islands 'P' and 'Q' turrets were fired across the deck to give 4 gun salvos in *Invincible*, but apart from deck damage this dazed and deafened gun-layers, trainers and sight-setters, and 'P' turret reported that the trainers had to be relieved constantly as they were too dazed to train properly. After the battle this cross-deck firing was acknowledged as a mistake, only to be used in emergency in future. The mountings in *Inflexible* and *Indomitable* were Mark BVIII as in the *Lord Nelson* and *Dreadnought* supplied respectively by Vickers and Elswick, and powered by the usual British hydraulic system, but *Invincible* originally had electric mountings, 'A' and 'Y' being Vickers Mark BIX and 'P' and 'Q' Elswick Mark BX. These were converted to hydraulic in 1914. The 12in guns fired an 850lb shell at 2725fs muzzle velocity (new gun 80°F) and the mountings allowed 13½° elevation giving a range with the original 2crh shells of 16350 yds increased to 19 000 yds when 4crh shells were supplied to these ships in 1915-16.

The original peace time outfit was 80 rounds per gun, 24 being APC, 40 CP, both black powder filled and 16 lyddite filled HE these proportions being maintained in the war outfit of 110 rounds per gun. With the supply of 4 crh shells the figures became 33 APC (lyddite filled, possibly some black powder), 38 CPC and 39 HE, altered by mid-1916 to 44 APC, 33 CPC, 33 HE. After Jutland it was recommended that the HE be reduced to 10 and then that the outfit should be half APC and half CPC. The final outfit after the war was 77 shellite filled APC and 33 CPC

TABLE 4: COMPARISON OF DESIGNED LEGEND WEIGHTS

CLASS	MINOTAUR	INDOMITABLE	DREADNOUGHT
Equipment (tons)	595 (4.1%)	660 (3.8%)	650 (3.6%)
Armament including turret shields	2065 (14.1%)	2440 (14.1%)	3100 (17.3%)
Machinery & Engineer's stores	2530 (17.3%)	3390 (19.7%)	2050 (11.5%)
Coal	1000 (6.9%)	1000 (5.8%)	900 (5.0%)
Armour & Protection	2790 (19.1%)	3460 (20.1%)	5000 (27.9%)
Hull	5520 (37.8%)	6200 (35.9%)	6100 (34.1%)
Board margin	100 (0.7%)	100 (0.6%)	100 (0.6%)
TOTAL (tons)	14 600	17 250	17 900

per gun. At times during the War a few shrapnel were also carried. A main armament director was fitted on the foremast in *Invincible* by early 1915 and in the other two later the same year.

The secondary anti-destroyer guns were originally to have been 12 pdr/18 cwt, probably 20 in number, but as a result of trials against the *Skate* in 1906, 16—4in/40 QF Mark III, firing a 25lb shell, on PI* mountings were adopted. The original distribution was 4 in the forward and 4 in the after superstructure and 8 on the turret crowns, but in 1914-15 the 4 guns on 'A' and 'Y' were mounted in the forward superstructure and in 1915 the 4 on 'P' and 'Q' were removed, reducing the number to 12. The 4in QF Mark III was not a powerful gun and in April 1917 *Indomitable* was rearmed with 12—4in/50 BL Mark VII on PVI mountings, *Inflexible* following in July 1917 with 12—4in/44 BL Mark IX on CPI mountings. Both these fired a 31lb shell and at least brought the 2 surviving ships of the class up to the standard of most of the other British battlecruisers in anti-destroyer guns. 100 rounds per gun (50 later 30 common, 50 later 70 HE) were carried for the QF IIIs, while *Indomitable* ultimately had 100 per gun (25 CP, 60 HE, 15 HE Night tracer) for the BLVIIs and *Inflexible* 150 per gun (37 CP, 90 HE, 23 HE Night tracer) for the BLIXs. A field mounting for a 4in QF Mark III was originally authorised with 200 rounds of shrapnel.

The 4in QF IIIs also served as saluting guns, and the usual 4—3pdr Hotchkiss were not fitted until 1919.

The AA armament was complicated. *Invincible* had 1—3in/20cwt Mark I in October 1914, but it was removed in November and replaced by a 3pdr Hotchkiss, the latter being retained when *Invincible* again had a 3in/20cwt Mark I in April 1915. Both guns were still in her when she was lost. *Inflexible* had 1—4in on 'A' and then 1 on 'X' converted to HA fire in October 1914 by her gunnery officer, the ingenious Commander Verner, and they were used for long range 'howitzer' fire at the Dardanelles in early 1915. This conversion was officially frowned on, and 1—3pdr Hotchkiss was added in November 1914 followed by 1—3in/20 cwt Mark 1 in July 1915. A 4in BL Mark VII on a 60° mounting replaced the Hotchkiss in August 1917, the 3in being retained. *Indomitable* had no AA guns until a 3in/20cwt Mark I was mounted in April 1915 and this was supplemented by a 60° 4in BL Mark VII in April 1917.

The 3pdr Hotchkiss were originally allowed 500 rounds of HE and the 3in 270 HE and 30 shrapnel, but these outfits were much reduced, the 3in finally having 120 HE and 30 incendiary and the 4in apparently 75 nose fuzed common and 75 shrapnel, though this was to be altered to 160 HE and 40 incendiary.

Aircraft
By the end of the War both surviving ships had 1 Sopwith Camel and 1 1½ Strutter with flying off platforms on 'P' and 'Q' turrets.

Torpedo tubes comprised 4 broadside and 1 stern submerged 18in for which 23 torpedoes were carried. The stern tube was removed from *Inflexible* and *Indomitable* in 1916. The above armament was good for a first attempt at a new type of ship though the 12in distribution was faulty and the original 4in guns too weak. The necessary protection had however been squeezed out by the demands of speed, high freeboard, armament and fuel capacity.

ARMOUR

The belt armour was 6in thick from a little forward of 'A' barbette to the centre line of 'X', being joined to the after face of the latter by a 6in angled bulkhead. At 26ft 0in draught it ran from 4ft 0in below to 7ft 3in above the waterline (ie to main deck level) and was continued to the stem but not aft at 4in. Otherwise the sides were unarmoured. The barbettes of 27ft internal diameter, had 7in to the main deck but only 2in between the main and armour decks except for the exposed after face of 'X' which was 7in. The turrets were 7in on face, sides and rear, where there was also a 6½in thick mild steel balancing weight, and had 3in roofs and rear floors. The 4in guns were unprotected originally, but were given shields during the war, and some of the openings in the superstructure plated in. The fore CT was 10—7in with 2in roof and floor, 3in on the signal tower and a 4in tube to the lower CT on the armour deck. The after CT was 6in with 2in roof and floor and a 3in tube to the after lower CT. The lower CTs were 2in on the sides, the main deck which formed the roof being 2in over the forward and 1in over the after one. Otherwise the main deck was ⅜in over the 4in bow belt and 2in below barbettes 'A', 'P' and 'Q'. After Jutland 1in was added in wake of all barbettes. The armour (lower) deck was 2in on the slopes and 1½in flat behind the 6in belt, 1½in forward and 2½in aft. The magazines were above the shell rooms, with their crowns formed by the armour deck and the ammunition spaces had some underwater protection from 2½in longitudinal screen bulkheads though there was little room by 'P' and 'Q' where the handing rooms abutted on the screen bulkheads. Apart from this, there was no special torpedo protection.

It is obvious from the foregoing that they were not able to withstand heavy projectiles but the loss of *Invincible* at Jutland was due to the behaviour of her propellant charges, and with German type charges she would in all probability have survived.

STABILITY

Metacentric height was determined as 3.8—3.85ft (*Minotaur* 2.95ft) at legend displacement rising to 4.22—4.25ft at deep load (no oil) (*Minotaur* 3.3ft) and to 5.13—5.15ft with oil fuel. By September 1917 calculated figures were respectively 3.63, 4.18, 4.71ft due to the increased top weight. The rolling period was about 14 seconds.

MACHINERY

There were 31 boilers, Babcock in *Indomitable*, and large tube Yarrow in the other two, working at 250lb/sq in. No 1 boiler room which was 52ft long had 7 boilers while Nos 2, 3 and 4, the latter aft of 'P' and 'Q', were 34ft long but wider and had 8 each. This compares with a total length of 160ft for the *Minotaur's* 5 boiler rooms housing 23 boilers. The 2 engine rooms were 76ft long (*Minotaur* 68ft) each containing one set of Parsons turbines, the high pressure ahead and astern being on the wing shafts, and the low pressure ahead and astern with a separate cruising turbine on the inner shafts. Designed shp was 41 000 = 25kts, which was comfortably exceeded, and legend fuel 1000 tons coal, maximum figures being *Indomitable* 3083 coal, 710 oil; *Inflexible* 3084 coal, 725 oil; *Invincible* 3000 coal, 738 oil. Official radii of action were 4480-4600 sea miles at 15kts and 2270-2340 at 23kts with coal only, increased to 6020-6110 and to 3050-3110 if full oil was carried — which was rarely the case. It should be noted that the oil was burnt by spraying into the coal fired furnaces, and separate oil fired boilers were not fitted in British mixed fuel ships, unlike the later German. Trials of British ships were normally run burning coal only.

On the measured mile all 3 ships exceeded 26kts, *Invincible* being the fastest with 46 500shp = 26.64kts at 295.2 mean rpm and a draught of 25ft 2in fore and 26ft 9½in aft. *Inflexible* recorded 46 947shp =26.48kts 291.3 mean rpm, and *Indomitable* 47 791shp =26.11kts and 296 mean rpm.

GENERAL

In appearance they were impressive ships with tripod fore and mainmasts, and 3 large funnels, and particular so after the fore-funnel had been raised in 1910 for *Indomitable* 1911 for *Inflexible* and early 1915 for *Invincible*.

A comparison of designed legend weights between the *Minotaur*, *Indomitable* and *Dreadnought* is instructive (see Table 4). The percentage figures show well the price in machinery weights for increased speed and to a lesser extent that of the long high freeboard hull. The legend armament percentage for the *Indomitable* is no greater than that for the *Minotaur*, in spite of the great improvement in efficacy, though it must be stated that the actual figure for the first named ship was 2551 tons or a percentage of 14.7 on her 17 410 tons normal displacement.

WAR SERVICE

In August 1914 *Inflexible* and *Indomitable*, along with *Indefatigable*, were in the Mediterranean, *Inflexible* as the flagship of the C in C, Admiral Sir A B Milne. On 4 August before the expiry of the time limit of the British ultimatum, the *Indomitable* and *Indefatigable* made contact with the German *Goeben*, a far more powerful ship. The *Goeben's* bottom had not been cleaned for 10 months, and she suffered from boiler tube troubles so that she could not do more than 24kts, with a sustained speed of 22½. This was, however, quite sufficient to get away from the 2 British ships, of which *Indomitable* was the slower. She had not been docked since March 1913, and a 4 months overdue refit at Malta was broken off just after it had

Indomitable, 1908
MoD (Navy)

H.M.S. "INDOMITABLE".

Invincible, 1910
MoD (Navy)

New Zealand and *Australia* leading *Indomitable.* Taken
from the Forth Bridge, 1918
IWM

begun, when war appeared imminent. She was thus very foul and although she had averaged 268 rpm on a 6 hour full power trial in May 1914, did not attain more than 240-249 when following the *Goeben*. *The Indomitable* had 2130 tons coal aboard when she lost touch, and it would seem that the 22kts usually credited to her on this occasion is somewhat optimistic.

The *Indefatigable* and *Indomitable* in company with the French pre-dreadnoughts *Suffren* and *Verité* bombarded the outer Dardanelles forts on 3 November. This was purely a demonstration, the two British ships expending 46—12in between them at 14 000—12 300yds, with only the *Indefatigable* achieving a noteworthy result. As far as the *Invincible* and *Inflexible* were concerned the **Battle of the Falkland Islands** was fought against Von Spee's two armoured cruisers *Scharnhorst* and *Gneisenau* though about 20 shells were fired initially at the light cruiser *Leipzig*. Both ships were sunk after a great fight against heavy odds at ranges of 16 000 to less than 8000yds and for most of the battle 12 000yds or more. The number of hits made on the 2 German ships is not known but was probably about 40 on each. The ammunition expenditure was very high, the *Invincible* firing 513—12in (128 APC, 259 CP, 126 HE) and the *Inflexible* 661 (157 APC, 343 CP, 161 HE) while the armoured cruiser *Carnarvon* (4—7.5in, 6—6in) also expended 85—7.5in and 60—6in virtually all at the *Gneisenau*. It may be noted that the total number of 12in shells fired by Togo's 4 battleships at Tsushima was only 446. Neither ship had directors, the installation in *Invincible* being incomplete. As far as can be determined the worst damage to the German ships was caused by shells striking below the waterline and hits on the 1in battery roof also caused much damage, the 12in shells having angles of descent of $17\frac{1}{2}°$ at 14 000yds and 24° at 16 350.

The *Invincible* was hit by 22 shells, of which 12 were 8.3in, 6—5.9in and 4 unidentified. There were 11 hits on the deck, 4 on the side armour, 4 on the unarmoured side, 1 below water, 1 on 'A' turret and 1 on the foremast, but only one man was slightly wounded.

The *Inflexible* was only hit 3 times with slight damage to the 4in guns on 'A' and 'X' turrets and had 1 killed and 3 wounded.

Both battlecruisers burnt oil fuel with their coal when chasing von Spee before the battle began, somewhat unskilfully in the case of *Invincible* whose dense black funnel smoke hampered her own gunners and *Inflexible's* during the action. *Invincible* however averaged 298 rpm for one hour and at one period reached 308. Her draught was 28ft fore and 30ft aft, and as her bottom had been newly coated before leaving England, she may well have made 26kts.

The two battlecruisers had certainly done their business at the Falkland Islands, but they made rather heavy work of it and it might well have been investigated why so many 12in shells had to be fired and why about 40 hits were needed to sink each armoured cruiser.

The Battle of the Dogger Bank on 24 January 1915 was the first time the rival battlecruisers had engaged each other. The *Indomitable* took part but she was the slowest of the 5 British ships and handicapped by 2 crh shells, so that she did not open fire till 113 minutes after the *Lion* and at a range of 16 250yds. Her target was the armoured cruiser *Blücher*, already crippled, and in an hour's firing at ranges down to about 6000yds the *Indomitable* expended 40 APC, 15 CP and 79 HE, in addition to 2 shrapnel at the airship *L5*. It is impossible to separate the damage she caused from that due to the *Tiger*, *Princess Royal* and *New Zealand* which also fired at the *Blücher* in the latter part of the battle. The *Indomitable* was hit by an 8.3in ricochet from her opponent with negligable damage. During the chase the *Indomitable* recorded 292 rpm, perhaps attaining 25kts and after the battle took the disabled *Lion* in tow and brought her to Rosyth with a screen which at one time totalled 55 destroyers.

The *Inflexible* was the next ship of the class to be in action, taking part in the naval attack on the **Dardanelles**, an employment which was most unlikely to have been considered by anyone concerned with her design. She was initially the flagship of the C in C Vice Admiral Carden and took part in the bombardment of the outer forts on 19 and 25 February 1915, firing 47 CP shells on the first occasion, and 10 (1 a premature) on the second. The *Inflexible* left for Malta on 10 March to shift over the 2—12in in 'A' turret which had fired a total of 213 and 183 rounds, and returned to take part in the major attack on the inner forts on 18 March. In this operation the *Inflexible* was one of the 4 ships that engaged the main forts at long range, as far as *Inflexible* was concerned 13 700—16 200yds, the others being *Queen Elizabeth*, *Agamemnon* and *Lord Nelson* with *Inflexible* nearest the Asiatic shore. Few less suitable duties for a very lightly armoured battlecruiser could be devised. The effective Turkish guns that could bear on the ships were 4—14in/35 (German notation), 13—9.4in/35, 3—6in/45, 5—5.9in/40, and 32—5.9in mobile howitzers. With 4 crh shells of which there were about 25 rounds per gun, the 14in could range to 19 000 and the 9.4in to 15 800yds. For all her unsuitability the *Inflexible* did better than any other ship, putting the 2—14in guns in Rumeli Hamidieh out of action for the day before they had fired a shot, from damage to the loading derrick in one and to the traversing mechanism in the other. Otherwise of the above effective guns only 1—9.4in was put out of action by the fleet.

The *Inflexible* appears to have fired 182—12in, most if not all CP, though the figures may include some HE. She was hit by a number of shells as given below, and also struck a mine, the only British battlecruiser to suffer mine or torpedo damage in the war. Her casualties were 33 killed and 13 wounded. Dealing first with the damage from shells:

1 A 14in burst close to the hull on the port side aft, driving in the plating for 33ft about 6ft below water along the line of the armour deck. Some compartments including the port provision room (40ft x 20ft maximum) were flooded giving a slight list to port.

2 9.4in burst on side above armour, hole about 2ft diameter.

3 9.4in hit foremast at level of flying bridge, causing a fire which completed the destruction of the foretop fire control (qv5).

4 5.9in howitzer hit left gun 'P' turret. The gun was considered out of action from cracks about 17ft from the muzzle.

INVINCIBLE CLASS APPEARANCE CHANGES

(Typical of modifications to the earlier British battlecruisers)

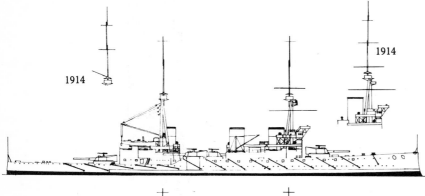

Invincible class as designed, 1905

Inflexible as completed, 1909

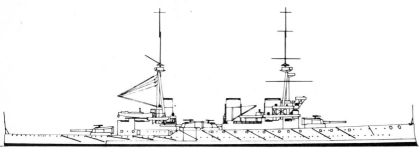

Invincible, 1913

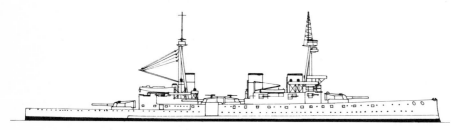

Invincible, December 1914

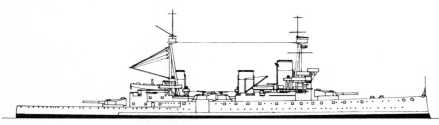

Indomitable, 1914/15

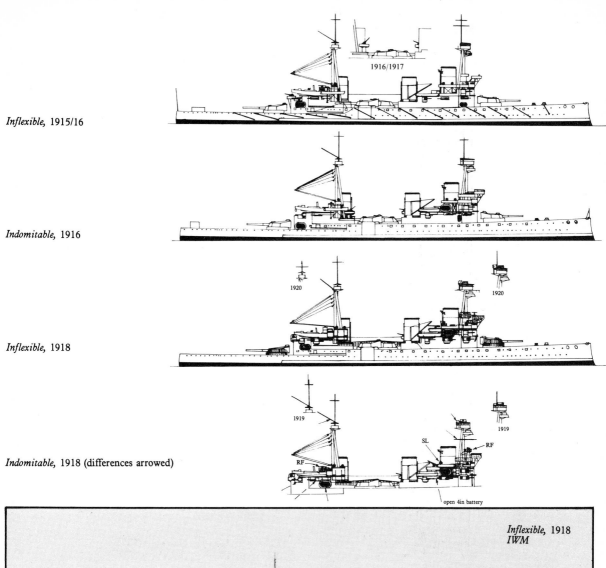

Inflexible, 1915/16

1916/1917

Indomitable, 1916

Inflexible, 1918

1920

1920

Indomitable, 1918 (differences arrowed)

1919

1919

SL

RF

RF

open 4in battery

Inflexible, 1918
IWM

5 Howitzer shell, thought to be 4in, struck signalling yard and burst on foretop roof, nearly all the complement there being casualties.

6 1 hit by small shell and 3 by shrapnel bursts. Minor damage only.

In addition a heavy shell sank *Inflexible's* picket boat.

The mine was one of 26 Carbonit mines (176lb charge) laid by the small steamer *Nusret* in the early hours of 8 March, which in addition to damaging *Inflexible*, sank the pre-dreadnought battleships *Irresistible*, *Ocean* and *Bouvet*. It exploded on the starboard bow by the after end of the fore torpedo flat just forward of 'A' and at platform deck level 17ft above the keel, making a hole 15 x 15ft with damage extending for a length of 36ft. The starboard side of the torpedo flat and the compartments below it were completely wrecked, and a locker full of Calcium phosphide Holmes' lights used for torpedo exercising and collision heads caught fire. All in the torpedo flat, apparently numbering 27, were killed. Electric light failed, ventilating fans stopped and nearly all emergency oil lamps went out. In 'A' magazine and shell room the men were thrown off their feet and both shell bogies overturned, while 'A' turret was felt to lift bodily, but the armour deck and magazine screen bulkhead prevented damage to the shell and magazine spaces, and practically confined the explosion to the submerged torpedo flat and compartments below it, though water entered the forward shell room and magazine, and later the lower conning tower. Some of the bulkheads strained badly, and the wounded were got into the cutter, but the *Inflexible* retired safely at 12kts. She was listing to starboard and her draught had changed from 30ft 3in forward, 30ft 8in aft, to 35ft 6in forward and 29ft aft, indicating that about 1600 tons of flood water were present, of which about 200 tons were due to the 14in near miss described above.

A 3in thick wood patch, stiffened by iron flats, was fitted over the whole and a concrete bulkhead built in the torpedo flat about 10ft from the side. After these temporary repairs she left Mudros on 6 April for Malta, arriving on 10 April. The voyage was not without incident, as on 7 April when steaming at 10kts the patch started to leak, and on the morning of 10 April the bulkheads began to complain at 5kts with a heavy sea on the starboard bow. It was impossible to steer going astern and the *Canopus* which was escorting her, had to tow the *Inflexible* stern-first for the last 8 hours before arrival at Malta during which time the patch washed away. The *Inflexible* was docked at Malta for further temporary repairs, and then left to be permanently repaired at Gibraltar, arriving on 24 April and leaving on 15 June to join the Grand Fleet. On the whole she has withstood the mine explosion as well as could be expected.

The Battle of Jutland was the other occasion on which the first battlecruisers were in action (31 May 1916) where for the first time all 3 were engaged together forming the 3rd Battlecruiser Squadron under Rear-Admiral The Hon H L A Hood with his flag in *Invincible*. It was also the first action in which they had the advantage of the longer ranging 4 crh shells. The 3rd BCS had been at Scapa for exercises and was ordered by Jellicoe to support the other battlecruisers under Beatty, which had come from Rosyth, soon after the latter were in action. Contact was however not made until shortly after that between Jellicoe and Beatty, but the unexpected appearance of Hood's small force from the eastward had a distracting effect on the Germans quite disproportionate to its weakness. The 3rd BCS first fired at the 2nd Scouting Group, the only modern light cruiser squadron with the German fleet, opening at 10 000yds. The *Wiesbaden* had both her engines permanently disabled by a shell from the *Invincible* and the *Pillau* had all her 6 coal fired boilers put out of action (3 permanently) by one from the *Inflexible* though she could do 24kts on her 4 oil fired boilers. The 3rd BCS then engaged the leading German battlecruisers at 8500-11 000yds in conditions where their opponents could for a time see virtually nothing, and it was then that they achieved the greatest British success of the whole battle by inflicting the damage which eventually proved fatal to the *Lützow*. This was caused by 2 shells which hit below water in or near the forward broadside torpedo flat, and the resultant flooding quickly put the *Lützow* out of action, but before this occurred, the visibility drastically changed, the *Lützow* and *Derfflinger* saw the *Invincible* clearly, and after about 4 hits which seem to have done little damage, a shell from the *Lützow* blew the roof off 'Q' turret, the flash of ignited propellant reached the magazine and the *Invincible* was broken in two, the bow and stern remaining above water for a time like two half-tide rocks. 1026 were lost in her, but apart from this, the fatal damage to the *Lützow* was far more important than the loss of the *Invincible*.

Altogether it is believed that 8 hits were made on the *Lützow* by the *Invincible* and *Inflexible*, mostly by the former, while the *Indomitable* made 3 on *Derfflinger* and 1 on *Seydlitz*. Subsequently the *Indomitable* and *Inflexible* joined astern of the other battlecruisers, *Indomitable* firing at the light cruiser *Regensburg* and both at German destroyers, while in the final daylight action *Indomitable* engaged *Seydlitz* and then the pre-dreadnought *Pommern* scoring a hit on the latter, while *Inflexible* seems to have fired at the *Moltke*. Next morning *Indomitable* fired 2 APC, loaded overnight, at the airship *L11*. Neither *Inflexible* nor *Indomitable* were hit during the battle.

The *Invincible* is thought to have fired about 110—12in shells, *Inflexible* fired 88 (10 APC, 59 CPC, 19HE) and *Indomitable* 175 (99 APC, 10 CPC, 66 HE) in addition to 4—4in. The two surviving ships were not in action again and were sold for scrapping in 1921.

CONCLUSIONS

As will be seen from the foregoing their war-time service was varied, and on the whole successful, though it was fortunate that they were only once engaged by up-to-date heavy guns, when *Invincible* was quickly sunk. Armour thick enough to keep out the German 12in shells would of course have saved her, but so in all probability would German type propellant charges. Otherwise the weak points shown in action were the lack of speed compared with other battlecruisers, the limitation of the broadside to 6 guns and the short range of the 2 crh shells. The indifferent effect of these and the not particularly accurate medium and long range shooting at the Falkland Islands, were not specific features in 1914.

INDEFATIGABLE CLASS
INDEFATIGABLE, AUSTRALIA, NEW ZEALAND

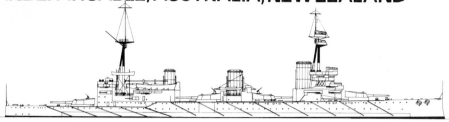

New Zealand, 1916

TABLE 5: INDEFATIGABLE CLASS PARTICULARS

Dimensions: 555ft (pp) 588ft (wl) 590 (oa) x 80ft x 26ft 6in mean.
Legend displacement: 18 750tons *Indefatigable*, 18 800 others.
Actual normal displacement (with fore and aft draught):   18 470tons (25ft 1in/26ft 9in) and 18 500 (24ft 9in/27ft 0in).
Deep load (less oil fuel):   21 240 tons for all three.
Sinkage: 75tons/inch, mean full load draught 30ft 0in.
Freeboard: 30ft forward, 22ft 3in amidships, 17ft 3in aft.

	Builder	Machinery	Laid down	Launched	Completed
INDEFATIGABLE	Devonport	Clydebank	23.2.1909	28.10.1909	.4.1911
AUSTRALIA	Clydebank	Clydebank	23.6.1910	25.10.1911	.6.1913
NEW ZEALAND	Fairfield	Fairfield	20.6.1910	1.7.1911	.11.1912

In chronological order the German *von der Tann* and *Moltke* should be considered next, but it is more convenient to deal first with the 3 remaining British 12in gunned ships. The *Invincible* class can be summed up in the words of the traditional old time schoolmaster 'good, but can do much better in future' — unfortunately as was so often the case, the hoped-for improvement was for the most part lacking.

DESIGN

The *Indefatigable* built under the 1908-9 programme, that is 3 years after the *Invincible,* was basically a similar ship modified to allow an 8 gun broadside for arcs of 70°, the limit of training of 'P' and 'Q' on the opposite beam. She was a distinctly inferior fighting ship to the *von der Tann* laid down in March 1908, and quite outclassed by the *Moltke* begun a month before the *Indefatigable.* There was still less reason for repeating the design with a few changes in the *New Zealand* and *Australia* built at the expense of the respective Dominions, and in the case of the former presented to the British Navy, as these two ships were not laid down until mid 1910, after the *Lion* and *Princess Royal* which were over 7500 tons larger (see Table 5).

ARMAMENT

12 inch. Book after book has credited these ships with 12in/50 calibre guns, but the main armament was 8—12in/45 cal Mark X guns as in the *Invincible,* the only difference being that 'P' and 'Q' turrets were more widely separated, being located to port forward and to starboard aft of the middle funnel. The arcs on the opposite beam were 'P' 40° forward, 30° aft; 'Q' 30° forward, 40° aft. Gun axis heights were as in the *Invincibles* and the mountings Mark B VIII* as in the *Bellerophon* class, supplied by Elswick for *Indefatigable* and *New Zealand* and by Vickers for *Australia.* The elevation was 13½° as in

BVIII, and the mountings were similar, as is shown by *Australia* later having 1 BVIII and 7 BVIII*: 4 crh shells were supplied initially and the original peace outfit of 80 rounds per gun was 24 APC, 28 CPC, 28 HE with in addition 6 shrapnel. The 110 rounds per gun war outfit was 33 APC, 38 CPC, 39 HE, subsequently altered as in the *Invincibles.* Main armament directors were fitted on the foremast in 1915-16.

The secondary anti-destroyer guns comprised 16—4in/50 BL Mark VII on PII* mountings, 6 in the forward and 10 in the after superstructure: 2 of the after guns were removed in November 1915. Another 4in was removed from *New Zealand* in 1917 and a further 4 guns in January 1919 before she took Lord Jellicoe on his Empire naval mission. The ammunition outfit was 100 rounds per gun, originally 50 common and 50 HE but later 30, 70 and finally 25 common, 60 HE and 15 HE night tracer. The 4—3pdr Hotchkiss saluting guns were removed in 1915 except in *Australia* which retained 2 as flagship of the 2nd Battlecruiser Squadron and in 1919 both she and *New Zealand* again had 4.

AA guns. *Indefatigable* had 1—3in/20 cwt Mark I AA gun added in March 1915 which was still mounted when she was lost. *Australia* also had 1—3in/20 cwt Mark I added in March 1915 and 1—4in BL Mark VII on a 60° mounting in June 1917. Both were replaced in January 1920 by 2—4in QF Mark V on 80° mountings. *New Zealand* had 1—3in/20cwt Mark I and 1—6pdr Hotchkiss mounted in October 1914. The 6pdr was removed in late 1915, and a 60° 4in BL Mark VII added in 1917, while in February 1919 the 3in was replaced by 2—2pdr pompoms. The 3in and 4in AA ammunition outfits were the same as for the *Invincible* class with initially 500 HE for the 6pdr and apparently 800 common nose fused and 200 CP (for use against MTBs)for the 2pdr.

Aircraft. By the end of the war *Australia* and *New Zealand* had flying off platforms on 'P' and 'Q' with 1 Camel and 1 1½ Strutter each. The first successful flying off of the 2-seater 1½ Strutter was from *Australia's* 'Q' platform on 4 April 1918.

Torpedo tubes were reduced to 2 broadside submerged 18in aft of 'X' barbette and 12 torpedoes were carried.

ARMOUR

The above armament shows some improvement in distribution of the 12in and a better type of 4in than was originally in the *Invincible*. The armouring was however in some ways worse. In *Indefatigable* the 6in belt extended for only 298ft amidships, and at 26ft 6in draught from 7ft 6in above to 3ft 6in below water, the weight devoted to the 6in belt and necessary armour bolts being reduced from 815 to 721 tons. By 'A' and 'X' the belt was only 4in running some way past 'A' but not beyond 'X', and was carried to the stem and stern at 2½in (2in on ½in shell plating) rising nearly to the upper deck near the bows, but not reaching the main deck aft. There were straight bulkheads at the outer ends of the 4in belt, the forward one being 4in between the armour and main decks, and 3in to the upper deck, and the after one 4½—4in between the armour and main decks. There was no upper side armour. The barbettes were 7in above the main deck, but below only 2in trunks to the armour deck, except for 'X' which was 7in reduced to 3in behind the 4in side. The turrets were 7in with 3in roofs as in *Invincible*, except that the roof supports were strengthened, which was a useful improvement. The 4in guns were unarmoured and the CT had 10in with 3in roof and floor and a 4in tube. The signal and spotting tower was 4-3in and the after CT (Torpedo control tower) only 1in. The funnel and ventilation uptakes had 1½—1in screens, as did the machinery hatches. The main deck was 1in over the 4in side armour and in way of the barbettes increased to 2in under 'A', 'P' and 'Q', and the lower (armour) deck 1½in with 2in slopes behind the 6in and 4in side except that it was reduced to 1in behind the foremost part of the 4in armour, and 2in forward and aft. The ammunition spaces had 2½in longitudinal screen bulkheads.

This very poor protection was modified in *Australia* and *New Zealand*. The 2½in bow and stern armour was removed and the belt increased to 5in by 'A' and 'X' and someway forward of 'A', with a length of 4in armour beyond, both forward and aft. The bulkheads at the end of the 4in side were both 4in to the main deck, the forward one being continued to the upper deck at 1½in. 'X' barbette was reduced to 4—3in between the main and armour decks, and the fore CT tube was 4—3in, with 6—3in on the spotting tower. The main deck was 1in between the 4in bulkheads, with 2in under 'A', 'P' and 'Q', while the armour deck was reduced to 1in behind the side armour and increased to 2½in at the ends, and the ammunition space screen bulkheads were 2½—1½in. Otherwise the armour was as in *Indefatigable*. As will be seen the small improvement in the side armour was accompanied by reductions elsewhere. After Jutland 1in was added to a large area of the armour deck between 'P' and 'Q', and 1in to the main deck in wake of the barbettes, the total weight amounting to 110 tons.

1 *Indefatigable*, 1913
CPL

2 *New Zealand*, 1918
NMM

STABILITY

Metacentric height was calculated as 3.5ft (*Indefatigable* 3.45ft) at legend displacement, 3.9ft at deep load without oil fuel and 4.8ft with oil, these figures being less than in the *Invincible* as originally completed.

MACHINERY

There were 32 Babcock boilers in 5 boiler rooms, Nos 1 and 2 which were each 38ft long having respectively 5 and 7, Nos 3 and 4 which were amidships between 'P' and 'Q', 20ft and 38ft long with 4 and 8 boilers, and No 5 which was aft, 38ft long and 8 boilers. The main machinery spaces were 84ft long, 8ft more than in the *Invincible* and divided into 2 engine and 2 condenser rooms with Parsons turbines arranged as in the *Invincibles* except that there were no separate cruising turbines. Designed shp was 43 000 in *Indefatigable* and 44 000 in the other two =25kts

1

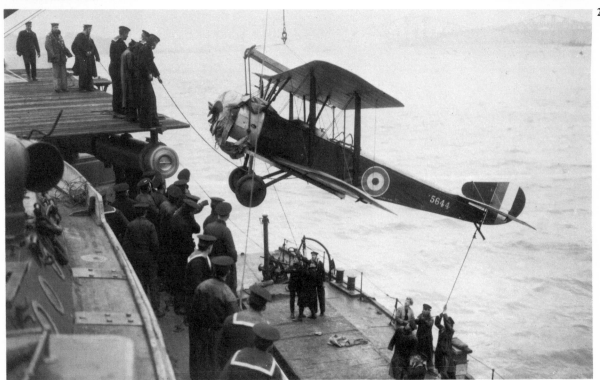

2

3

1 *Australia* coaling, 1918
2 *Australia,* Sopwith Pup being hoisted inboard, 1918
  IWM
3 *Australia* as completed
  CPL

while legend fuel was 1000 tons coal, and maximum 3340 coal and 870 oil in *Indefatigable,* with 3170 and 840 tons in the others. Official radius of action figures with coal only were respectively 5100 and 4770 at 16kts and 2470 and 2290 at 23kts increased with full oil to 6970, 6540, 3360 and 3140 sea miles.

Indefatigable's trials on the mile off Chesil Beach in December 1910 were run in bad weather and her propellers were not ideal, so that her first series only produced 44 596 shp =24.44kts at 288.5 rpm which was improved in the second series to 49 675 shp = 25.01kts at 299.1 rpm. This was far from satisfactory and in April 1911 she was tried with new propellers on the mile at Polperro in good weather. Instructions were given that the

usual trial conditions for forcing boilers could be exceeded, and at 25ft 9in forward 27ft 3in aft she recorded 55 140 shp = 26.89kts at 315.3 mean rpm. A report from the Admiralty Experimental works at Haslar in the ship's cover indicates that the shp was incorrectly measured and was actually higher.

New Zealand and *Australia* gave less trouble, and their mile figures were respectively 49 048 shp =26.385 kts, 299.68 mean rpm and 55 881 shp = 26.89kts 308.6 mean rpm. Subsequently at the Dogger Bank battle *New Zealand* was worked up to 316 rpm for over 2 hours and again for over an hour with a maximum of 320 and according to her torque meters attained 65 250 shp.

GENERAL

Although they had tripod fore and main masts like the *Invincible* class, the separation of the first two funnels gave them a quite distinct and less formidable appearance. The legend weights compared with *Indomitable's* were:

TABLE 6: **COMPARISON OF DESIGNED LEGEND WEIGHTS**

SHIP	INDOMITABLE	INDEFATIGABLE	AUSTRALIA
Equipment (tons)	660 (3.8%)	680 (3.6%)	680 (3.6%)
Armament including turret shields	2440 (14.1%)	2580 (13.8%)	2615 (13.9%)
Machinery & Engineer's stores	3390 (19.7%)	3655 (19.5%)	3655 (19.5%)
Coal	1000 (5.8%)	1000 (5.3%)	1000 (5.3%)
Armour & Protection	3460 (20.1%)	3735 (19.9%)	3670 (19.6%)
Hull	6200 (35.9%)	7000 (37.4%)	7070 (37.6%)
TOTAL inc 100 tons margin	17 250	18 750	18 790

It will be noted that the legend displacement for *Austrialia* is 10 tons down on the usual figure. It is not known where the discrepancy lies. There was a slight decrease in the percentage given to armament and to protection, and a larger rise in that absorbed by the high freeboard hull, not a satisfactory state of affairs.

WAR SERVICE

Their wartime service was less varied than that of the *Invincible's*.

Australia was originally employed in the Pacific and did not join the Grand Fleet until February 1915, too late for the Dogger Bank battle, while a collision with the *New Zealand* in fog on 22 April 1916 kept her out of Jutland.

Indefatigable followed the *Goeben* in company with the *Indomitable* as previously noted, and though she proved faster than the latter, could not keep in touch with the German ship. The *Indefatigable* recorded 272—278 rpm and about 1¼ hours before losing touch had 2560 tons coal aboard. It is doubtful if she exceeded 23kts at the best, and may well have not reached this speed. She also took part with the *Indomitable* in the short bombardment of the outer Dardanelles forts on 3 November 1914, and her last 2 shells at the old Sedd el Bahr fort hit the roof of the central magazine, pierced 6½ft of earth and 3¼ft of masonry and 10½ tons of black prismatic powder with 360 shells from 9.4in to 11in went up. The guns in the fort were buried under debris and 85 of the garrison killed and 23 wounded. No such result was achieved in all the long 1915 attack on the Dardanelles. She was next in action at the Battle of Jutland where she was blown up by the *von der Tann* in a duel lasting 14 or 15 minutes, with the loss of all but 2 of her complement of 1019. The *Indefatigable* was the rear ship of Beatty's 6 battlecruisers, and owing to the approach formation adopted was nearly bows on to the German line initially and was probably believed to be out of range. She was thus 3 or 4 minutes later in opening fire than the *von der Tann* and made no hits from about 40—12in shells fired. The *Indefatigable* is thought to have been hit once early in the action, and was then struck by 2 shells near 'X' barbette. An explosion followed and she began to sink by the stern. She was hit by 2 more shells, one on the forecastle and one on 'A' turret which appeared to explode on impact, and after an appreciable interval blew up. Whatever the cause of the final explosion, it was one in 'X' magazine that sank her. Just what happened is not known, but an 11in shell at 15 500—16 000yds could easily have gone through the 7/16in main deck side, the 1in main deck and the 3in armour of 'X' barbette, indicating the folly of thinning the armour of barbette bases where behind side armour.

New Zealand's war time service was all in the North Sea. At the Dogger Bank the *New Zealand* developed a surprising shp as described above and in spite of the heavy fuel load with which the battlecruisers put to sea, was at times in all probability exceeding 26kts and managed to keep up with the *Princess Royal*, though not with the *Lion* and *Tiger* during the chase. She was however not in range of the rear German ship, the *Blücher*, until 43 minutes after the action started and it is by no means certain that she scored any hits in the next 55 minutes before the *Blücher* began to fall astern. The number of hits which the *New Zealand* made in the final action against the *Blücher* cannot be determined but her total expenditure for the battle was 147—12in shells (8 CPC, 139 HE).

At Jutland the *New Zealand* fired more heavy shells than any other ship in either fleet, 420-12in (172 APC, 76 CPC, 172 HE) but the results were meagre. During the 'Run to the South' her targets were *Moltke* and *von der Tann*, and subsequently various ships that are difficult to identify, except for 2 salvos at destroyers, until the final daylight action when in succession the *New Zealand* fired at a dreadnought of the 1st Squadron, the *Seydlitz* and the pre-dreadnoughts *Schleswig Holstein* and *Schlesien*. No hits can be credited to her until the final action when she made 3 on *Seydlitz* and 1 on *Schleswig Holstein*. Her gunnery was not necessarily worse than that of Beatty's other battlecruisers as her 12in Mark X guns were inferior in accuracy to the excellent 13.5in Mark V, and in the final action when the range fell below 10 000yds, the *New Zealand* began to score. The *New Zealand* was hit once at Jutland, the only time in the war, by an 11in from *von der Tann* on 'X' barbette above the upper deck. The shell burst outside displacing a piece of the 7in armour, and jamming the turret for a short time, while shell fragments holed the 1in main deck. She was not in action again and was sold for scrapping in December 1922, while the *Australia* was scuttled with all due ceremony off Sydney on 12 April 1924.

New Zealand, 1914
NMM

VON DER TANN

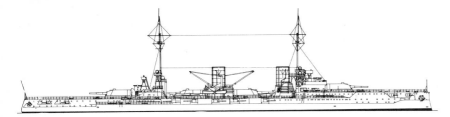

Von der Tann, as completed

TABLE 7: VON DER TANN PARTICULARS

Dimensions: 562ft 8in (wl) 563ft (oa) x 87ft 2½in x 26ft 6¾in mean.
Normal displacement: 19 064 tons.
Deep load displacement: 21 082 tons (however mean draught of 29ft 8in indicates around 21 700 tons).
Freeboard: 26½ft forward, 19ft amidships and aft, at normal displacement.

This ship, the first German battlecruiser, was a considerably better fighting ship than any of the British 12in battlecruisers. Design work took from August 1906 to June 1907, and she was laid down as 'F' under the 1907-8 programme on 25 March 1908 by Blohm and Voss who were also responsible for the machinery. She was launched on 20 March 1909 and commissioned for trials 1 September 1910, completing these 20 February 1911.

ARMAMENT

The main armament consisted of 8-11in SkL/45 in 4 twin turrets, forward and aft on the centre line and 2 echelonned amidships. In German ships with the latter arrangement the starboard wing turret was always forward of the port one, the reverse to British practice, and in the *von der Tann* the wing turrets were further inboard than in the *Invincibles* and *Indefatigables* and each had theoretical arcs of 125° on the opposite beam. The gun axis was well above deck, heights above lwl being 32ft 6in for the fore turret and 25ft 4in for the others. The 11in guns fired a 666lb shell with an 80° F charge temperature muzzle velocity of 2835 fs and with the type of shell in use during 1914-18, ranged 22 400yds at 20° elevation. The mountings were DrhLC/1907, electrically trained and elevated, and otherwise only used for the centreline turrets in *Posen* and *Rheinland*. As in most other turrets they had the working chamber and lower hoists as part of the revolving structure. As was often the case in the German ships the location of shell rooms and magazines varied from turret to turret. In the fore turret, the shell rooms were on the platform deck with the magazines above them on the lower deck, the armour deck being at middle deck level between end barbettes. For the after turret the positions were reversed, and for the wing turrets the magazines were on the platform deck and the shell rooms below on the hold. The outfit was 660 rounds for the 8 guns and only APC was carried. The German 'director-pointer' differed from the British director in being designed for the training of the guns only and not for elevation as well. It was fitted in the gunnery control tower for main and secondary armament in *von der Tann* by the middle of June 1915.

The secondary armament of 10-5.9in SKL/45 in MPLC/1906 mountings was in a main deck battery between the fore funnel and mainmast. It was intended to engage all kinds of ship targets and the 150 rounds per gun comprised APC and both base and nose fused HE, though latterly APC was not carried. The guns could range to 14 800yds or with the better shaped shell available in 1916 to 16 300yds., There were also 16-3.45in SKL/45 in MPLC/1906 mountings distributed equally between the forward and after superstructures, the upper deck far forward and the main deck far aft. 200 rounds per gun of HE with internal, nose and time and percussion fuzes were provided. The 4 guns in the after superstructure were replaced in early 1916 by 2-3.45in Flak L/45 in 70° MPLC/1913 mountings, and by the end of 1916, the 12 remaining 'low angle' 3.45in had been removed. There were 4-18in TT all submerged—1 bow, 1 stern and 2 broadside forward of 'A' barbette and of the torpedo bulkhead, and 11 torpedoes were carried.

ARMOUR

The above armament was perfectly adequate for dealing with the British 12in battlecruisers, and the *von der Tann* was far better protected. The main belt ran from the forward edge of the fore turret to a little past the after one and for a height of 49in of which 14in were below the legend wl, it was 10in thick tapering to 6in at the main deck and at the lower edge 5ft 3in below lwl. Straight 7in max bulkheads terminated the main belt, and the side armour was continued to the bows at 4¾in with 4in upper edge, and then at 4in. Aft the side armour ended in a 4in max bulkhead, about 10ft from the stern, and was 4in with 3.2in upper edge a little below the main deck. The battery armour was 6in with 0.8in screen and rear splinter bulkheads. The barbettes had an internal diameter of 26ft 7in (ball track 22ft 8in) and were 8in above the hull armour except that the outer face of the fore barbette was 9in and the inner face of this and the after barbette 6¾in. Behind the main belt and battery armour they were however drastically reduced to 1.2in. The turrets had 9in faces and rears, 7in sides, 3½in sloping front roofs, 2.4in flat roofs and 2in rear floors, while the fore CT was 10in with a 3.2in roof and the after CT 8in and 2in.

The flat part of the armour deck was at middle deck level behind the main belt and 1in thick with high 2in slopes. Forward it was flat at lower deck level and 2in thick, and it was also lowered aft where it was 3.2in on the flat part with 2-1in slopes. The main deck was 1in over the main belt outside the battery, and the upper deck 1in over the battery, while the forecastle deck was thickened to 0.9in round the fore barbette.

The torpedo bulkhead ran for the same length as the main belt, and was set about 13ft inboard amidships and was 1.2-1in thick. The space outboard was divided approximately in half by a thin longitudinal bulkhead, the outer part being empty and the inner filled with coal. This was the usual German torpedo protection system and against 1914-1918 underwater weapons was very effective.

STABILITY

Metacentric height was 6.92ft presumably at normal displacement, and Frahm anti-rolling tanks were fitted after construction was well advanced so that they had to be located further from the side than was ideal. With 231 tons of water in the tanks the roll was reduced from 17° to 11°, but they were later used to take abut 200 tons of extra coal, and bilge keels were fitted instead. The period of roll was about 11 seconds.

MACHINERY

There were 18 Schulz-Thornycroft (German 'Navy type') small tube boilers working at 235lb/sq in in 10 boiler rooms, the 2 foremost having one boiler each and the rest two, and 2 sets of Parsons turbines driving 4 shafts, the first use of turbines in a large German warship. The port forward engine room contained a high pressure ahead turbine on the wing shaft and the medium pressure cruising turbine on the inner, the starboard forward engine room differing in that the high pressure cruising turbine was on the inner shaft. Both the after engine rooms contained a high pressure astern turbine on the wing shaft and a low pressure ahead and astern in one casing on the inner shaft. The rotor drums of the main high pressure ahead turbines were 82½in diameter and those of the low pressure 115 to 111in. Designed shp, always a nominal figure in German battlecruisers was 43 600 giving 24¾kts at 280 rpm and normal coal was 984 tons and max 2760 excluding that in the former Frahm tanks. This gave a radius of action of about 2500 sea-miles at 22½kts or of 4400 at 14kts. Subsequently provision was made for spraying tar oil on the coal in the boiler furnaces and about 200 tons was carried.

German battlecruisers were always heavily forced on the mile during trials, and the von der Tann achieved 79 000 shp = 27.4kts at 324 rpm. In 1911 after a cruise to South America she covered the 1913 miles between Teneriffe and Heligoland at an average speed of 24kts, but she seems to have been liable to turbine troubles during the war.

GENERAL

She was the only German ship where the officers were accommodated forward. Scuttled at Scapa Flow on 21 June

TABLE 8:
COMPARISON OF LEGEND WEIGHTS

SHIP	VON DER TANN	INDEFATIGABLE
Hull (tons)	6004 (31.5%)	7000 (37.4%)
Machinery	3034 (15.9%)	3655 (19.5%)
Armour & Protection	5693 (29.8%)	3735 (19.9%)
Armament inc turret shields	2604 (13.7%)	2580 (13.8%)

1919, she was raised 7 December 1930 and broken up at Rosyth in 1931-1934. It had originally been intended to complete her with lattice masts but this was not done, and the von der Tann had pole fore and mainmasts.

It is always a process liable to error to compare the legend weights of ships of two different navies, but the following figures even if not absolutely comparable indicate why the von der Tann was a much better fighting ship than the Indefatigable (see Table 8).

WAR SERVICE

In the Battle of Jutland, the von der Tann was the rear ship in the 1st Scouting Group, and as previously related blew up the Indefatigable in the first 14 or 15 minutes, during which she fired 52 — 11in and 38 — 5.9in shells, at ranges varying between 13500 and 16000yds and is believed to have made 5 — 11in hits. She then engaged the New Zealand but shifted for 6 minutes to the Barham, before again firing at the New Zealand. The reason for diverting her fire from the far more formidable Barham to the New Zealand was that the 2 centre line turrets had been put out of action from hits, and only 2 guns would bear on the Barham continually as the von der Tann was zig-zagging to avoid the 15in salvos of the 5th Battle

Squadron. The starboard wing turret then broke down as the guns failed to run out properly when hot, and just before the end of the 'Run to the South', the right gun of the port wing turret followed suit. In this period the *von der Tann* fired 59 — 11in at the *New Zealand* at 14 000 to at least 20 000 yds, and 34 — 11in at the *Barham* at 17 000 to 18 600yds, scoring one hit on each.

After the 1st Scouting Group turned north, the *von der Tann* fired 10 — 11in from her one remaining gun at the *Malaya* at 18 200 to over 22 000yds, followed by 6 — 11in at a destroyer (either the *Onslow* or *Moresby*) the right gun of the port wing turret working again in this last spell of firing, and then both guns failing to run out so that for 1¼ hours the *von der Tann* had no heavy guns at all. The port wing turret was put right by 18.30, the starboard wing an hour later and then the after turret with hand training, elevation and lower hoists, so that in the final daylight action she could fire 9 — 11in and 15 — 5.9in shells at 9 600 — 12 000yds. Altogether the *von der Tann* expended 170 — 11in and 98 — 5.9in in the battle, the balance of the latter against destroyers. It was unfortunate for the Germans that her two wing turrets failed as the 20° elevation gave her the longest range of any of the 1st Scouting Group, and this would have been useful during the 'Run to the North'. In addition to turret troubles inferior coal caused excessive clinkering in the boiler furnaces, and by the end of the day her speed was reported as down to 18kts until fires were cleaned.

The *von der Tann* was hit 4 times. A 15in CPC from the *Barham* at about 19 000yds burst on the joint between the 4in and 3.2in plates of the side armour aft which was broken and distorted. Over 1000 tons of water entered the ship giving a list of 2° to starboard. Later on a 15in APC from the *Revenge* burst on the ventilation shaft abaft the

after CT, and splinters and debris together with smoke and gas entered the starboard after engine room via the ventilation trunks.

The other 2 hits were by 13.5in APC from the *Tiger* which was firing at the *von der Tann* in error. The first burst near the upper edge of the fore barbette on the 8in armour making a hole 35in x 22in. A large piece of armour flew in and jammed the turret for the rest of the battle: the range was about 17 000yds.

The second hit from the *Tiger*, 3 minutes after the first, demonstrated almost to perfection, the greatest weaknesss of the *von der Tann's* armouring, the drastic thinning of the barbette bases behind side armour. The shell went through the unarmoured side, the 1in main deck and 2 unarmoured bulkheads and burst 40in below the main deck in front of the after barbette, here only 1.2in thick. A hole about 12ft × 7½ft max was made, and the barbette forced against the ring bulkhead which was distorted, jamming the turret for 3½ hours, while splinters put the power training and elevating gear and the drive for the lower hoists out of action. Much damage was done to light structures, and the magazine flooding valves were buried under wreckage. A fire was started among the practice targets stowed below the turret, and dense smoke and gas entering through torn ventilation trunks, made both steering engine rooms untenable for 20 minutes. The fire continued to smoulder for some hours and enveloped the ship in smoke. No ammunition was ignited by this hit and 2 main and 2 fore charges in the working chamber and only 6 or 7ft from where the barbette was holed, were undamaged.

The *von der Tann* was repaired in dry dock at Wilhelmshaven after the battle, but she was not ready until 2nd August, as the fore turret proved defective when fired. Her casualties at Jutland were 11 killed and 15 wounded.

MOLTKE CLASS
MOLTKE, GOEBEN

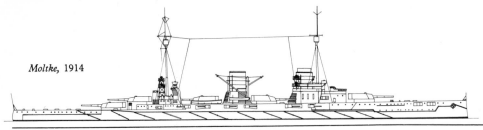

Moltke, 1914

TABLE 9: **MOLTKE AND GOEBEN PARTICULARS**

Dimensions: 610ft 3in (wl) 611ft 11in (oa) x 96ft 9½in x 26ft 11in mean.
Normal displacement,   22 616 tons
Deepload displacement: 25 000 (this appears to be about 300 tons too light for the mean draught of 29ft 5½in).
Freeboard: About 24ft forward, 14ft aft at normal displacement.

	Laid down	Launched	Commissioned for trial	Completed trials
MOLTKE	7.12.1908	7.4.1910	30.9.1911	31.3.1912
GOEBEN	28.8.1909	28.2.1911	2.7.1912	28.8.1912

DESIGN

Although the *von der Tann* had been a good first effort, the next German battlecruisers were much improved, and the British mistake of making no marked advance between the *Invincible* and the *Indefatigable* was avoided. Design work on the *Moltke,* known as 'G' before launching and built under the 1908-9 programme took from April 1907 to September 1908, and she and her sister ship of the next year's programme, the *Goeben,* 'H' before launching, were both built by Blohm & Voss, who were also responsible for the machinery.

It will be seen that although laid down before the *Indefatigable,* the *Moltke* was completed well after her, while the *Goeben* was completed after the *Lion,* the first of the next generation of British battlecruisers, although laid down before her. The hull form differed from that of the *von der Tann,* having more beam amidships and finer ends, while the forecastle deck was continued to aft of the main mast, though freeboard at bow and stern was reduced. The rise of floor forward was much sharper, and the stem was nearly straight instead of the slight ram bow of the *von der Tann.* Tandem rudders were also fitted instead of twin as in *von der Tann* or single in *Blücher.*

ARMAMENT

The main armament was increased to 10 — 11in SKL/50 in 5 twin turrets, the after turret in *von der Tann* being replaced by a superfiring pair. The arcs for the wing barbettes on the opposite beam were as in *von der Tann,* and the gun axis heights above lwl were for the forward turret 28ft 10in; beam turrets 27ft 8in; after turrets 28ft 3in and 20ft 5in. The 11in SKL/50 was very similar to the SKL/45, but lengthened 5 calibres at the muzzle which gave another 82ft per sec muzzle velocity. The mountings were Drh LC/1908, similar to the C/1907s in *von der Tann*

but only allowing 13½° elevation which limited the range to 19 500yds. After Jutland the elevation of *Moltke's* guns was increased to 16° for 21 300yds, and by the end of the war 22½° had been given to *Goeben's* 11in which would allow them to range to 25 300yds, the figure of 23 730 given in some British reports probably refering to the current range of *Goeben's* somewhat worn guns. This additional elevation was intended to prevent the *Goeben* being seriously outranged by the Russian *Imperatritsa Ekaterina* in the good visibility common in the Black Sea. The ammunition outfit is given as 81 APC per gun, though British Intelligence figures allow this for the 4 wing guns and 96 per gun for the 6 centreline ones. In all turrets the shell rooms were on the platform deck with the magazines above. Director pointers for the main and secondary armament were fitted to *Moltke* in the first half of 1915 and to *Goeben* in late 1916 or 1917.

The 5.9in and 3.45in guns and mountings were of the same pattern as in *von der Tann* but the numbers and disposition were altered. There were 12 — 5.9in in an upper deck battery running from the foremast to a little forward of the main mast, and originally 12 — 3.45in, 4 near the bows on the upper deck, 2 in the forward and 4 in the after superstructure and 2 on the upper deck aft of the 5.9in battery. The outfit was 150 rounds per gun for the 5.9in, and 250 for the 3.45in. In May 1915 the No 4 Port and Starboard 5.9in were removed from the *Goeben* for mounting in the In Tepe position on the Asiatic side of the Dardanelles; one was lost in transit, and in January 1916 the other which had been wrecked by a premature, was replaced by a further gun from the *Goeben.* The first two were not replaced in the *Goeben,* but the third was subsequently, by a gun sent from Germany. The 3.45in were reduced to 8 in both ships, by the removal of the 4 bow guns which were washed out at high speed, and then to 4, the after superstructure guns making way for 4 —

3.45in Flak L/45 (in *Goeben* the after superstructure guns
went to In Tepe in May 1915). By the end of 1916 the last
4 had been removed.

The torpedoes were 20in with 4 submerged TT (1
bow, 1 stern, 2 broadside forward) and 11 torpedoes were
carried.

ARMOUR

The main armourbelt extended between the outer edge of
the end barbettes and was $10\frac{3}{4}$in thick from 4ft 7in above to
1ft 2in below the legend waterline, tapering to 5.1in at the
lower edge 5ft 9in below lwl. The upper part of the belt
was a uniform 8in to the battery port sills or to the upper
deck outside the battery. Above the port sills the latter had
6in armour with similar bulkheads and 0.8in screens and
rear splinter bulkheads. Forward the belt was $4\frac{3}{4}$in and
then 4in, not reaching the upper deck except near the
stem, and aft it was 4in to about a third of the distance
between main and upper decks, ending in a 4in bulkhead
about 10ft from the stern. The bulkheads at the ends of the
main belt were straight and 8in maximum.

The barbettes were 8in except for the outer face of the
forward one which was 9in, but the wing barbettes were
reduced to 3.2in behind the 6in battery armour and all to
1.2in behind the 8in upper belt. The ball track and
internal diameters were the same as in *von der Tann*. The
turrets had 9in faces and rears, 7in sides, $3\frac{1}{2}$in sloping front
roofs, 2.4in flat roofs and 2in rear floors, the fore CT 14 —
10in with 3.2in roof and the after CT 8in with 2in roof.
The forecastle deck was 1in over the battery, the upper
deck 1in between the main and battery bulkheads, and the
armour deck, which was at main deck level amidships, 1in
on the flat with a high 2in slope. It was lowered forward
and aft where it was respectively 2in flat and 3.2in flat with
a 2in slope. Underwater protection was on the lines of the

von der Tann, but the torpedo bulkhead was 1.2in
increased to 2in by the ammunition spaces.

STABILITY

It was originally intended to use Frahm anti-rolling tanks,
and metacentric height was very large at 9.87ft,
presumably at legend displacement.

MACHINERY

There were 12 boiler rooms with 24 Schulz-Thornycroft
boilers working at 235lb/sq in and 2 sets of Parsons
turbines in 4 engine rooms. The high pressure turbines
were on the outer shafts in the forward engine rooms, and
the low pressure on the inner shafts in the after ones. Rotor
diameters were respectively 78in and 120in. The nominal
designed shp was $52\,000 = 25\frac{1}{2}$kts at 260 rpm, and normal
coal 984 tons with 3050 max giving a radius of action of
2370 sea miles at 23kts and 4120 at 14. About 200 tons of
tar oil was later carried for spraying on the coal in the
boiler furnaces. When tried on the measured mile *Moltke*
averaged 85 780 shp = 28.4kts at 332 rpm, and *Goeben*
85 660 = 28.0kts at 330 rpm.

GENERAL

Both ships had pole masts throughout their careers. *Moltke*
was scuttled at Scapa Flow 21 June 1919, salved in 1927
and broken up in 1927-29, while *Goeben* which spent the
1914-18 war as a nominally Turkish ship the *Yavuz Sultan
Selim,* was transferred to Turkey, thoroughly repaired and
refitted by Penhôet of St Nazaire at Ismit from 1926 to
1930, and not scrapped until 1971.

These were formidable ships for their day and far
superior to the British 12in battlecruisers. Their greatest
weakness in distribution of armour was the sharp reduction
in the barbettes where behind side armour.

Goeben, 1911
Drüppel

WAR SERVICE

In the **Dogger Bank battle** on 24 January 1915 the *Moltke* was second ship in the German line, and it is doubtful if she was ever fired at, certainly not for long, and no hits were made on her. Her target was initially the *Tiger*, for most of the battle the *Lion*, and finally the *Tiger*. Altogether 16 — 11in or 12in hits were made on the *Lion* and 6 on the *Tiger* and it seems probable that at least 8 or 9 of the 22 were from the *Moltke*. She fired 276 — 11in APC mostly at 16 000 — 18 000yds, and also 14 — 5.9in HE at 13 000 — 14 000yds at destroyers.

The *Moltke* was part of the covering force in the **Gulf of Riga operations** in 1915, and on 19 August she was hit by an 18in torpedo from one of *E1's* beam tubes. This hit on the starboard side far forward and only the bow torpedo flat and neighbouring compartments were flooded with 430 tons water on board. Two or three warheads were wrecked and the TNT-Hexanite filling scattered without ignition. She could still do 18kts, passed through the Kiel canal on 22 August and was repaired in a floating dock at Hamburg by Blohm and Voss, being ready for service on 20 September.

In the **Battle of Jutland** the *Moltke* was the fourth ship in the 1st Scouting Group, and initially her shooting was the best of any ship, as she scored 9 hits on the *Tiger* in the first 12 minutes at about 15 500 to 13 500yds and put two turrets out of action temporarily. A further 4 hits were made on the *Tiger* in the next half hour but no more afterwards. The *Moltke* subsequently fired at various ships of which the *New Zealand* and *Malaya* can be identified with certainty, but had no success. She expended 359 — 11in APC in the battle, and also 75 base-fused and 171 nose-fused 5.9in HE at the *Tiger* and various destroyers.

The *Moltke* also fired 4 torpedoes at the *Queen Mary* when the latter was well out of range.

She was the only German battlecruiser in good fighting order at the end of the day, and served as Hipper's flagship from 21.05 onwards. In spite of 4 — 15in hits and 1 — 13.5in near miss, as well as earlier clinkering troubles and the tar oil supplementary firing being choked by sediment, the *Moltke* was still able to do 25kts. The hits on her were:

13.5in near-miss from *Tiger* — burst below water forward, forcing skin plating in with some flooding.

15in all from *Barham* and *Valiant*.

1 Pierced 8in side armour at about 18 000yds below No 5 starboard 5.9in and burst in an outer bunker. No 5 gun was put out of action and the ready ammunition caught fire killing all 12 in the casemate. Flash passed down the hoist to the magazine badly burning 2 men. This shell was apparently an APC and one of the few British ones to behave as it should.

2 Passed through the ship and struck the 4in after armour on the reverse side. A plate was detached and flooding occurred above the armour deck for nearly 120ft.

3 Burst on $10\frac{3}{4}$in armour belt which was driven in 8in at the 5.1in thick lower edge. The skin plating below was bulged and torn with flooding of the wings for 71ft and also of some bunkers.

4 Similar to No 3 but rather more effect as the heavy armour was driven in 12in at the after end of the plate. Damage to skin plating and flooding were similar to No 3. The range for these last 2 hits was 16 500 — 15 500yds.

About 1000 tons of water were present in the ship as a result of these 5 shells. Casualties were 17 killed and 23 wounded.

The *Moltke* was first docked in a dry dock at

not serve with the 1st Scouting Group, and her career in the Mediterranean and Black Sea was by far the most eventful of any 1914-1918 capital ship. The *Goeben* was sent to the Mediterranean on 6 November 1912, her trials having been hurried through, and by mid 1914 she was much reduced in speed by leaky boiler tubes, and was to be replaced by the *Moltke* in October 1914. After the Sarajevo assassination on 28 June 1914, repairs were undertaken at Pola and by the outbreak of war 4460 new boiler tubes had been fitted with the help of dockyard workers from Germany. As described previously she was then quite fast enough to get away from the shadowing *Indomitable* and *Indefatigable* on 4 August, although at times 3 boilers were out of action together, and one man died in the bunkers from exhaustion. The *Goeben* entered the Dardanelles on 10 August 1914 and with the aid of boilermakers sent out from Germany, retubing was completed in late October 1914.

Her first operation in the Black Sea was the **bombardment of Sevastopol** on 29 October 1914. The Goeben fired for 15 minutes at 8500-13 000yds expending 47 — 11in and 12 — 5.9in without much success as far as is known, suffering 3 hits on the after funnel at near the *Goeben's* minimum range. On her return the *Goeben* seriously damaged the small destroyer *Lt Pushkin* by 2 — 5.9in shells at 11 000-13 500yds, and disposed of the minelayer *Pruth* which may have been scuttled under the *Goeben's* 5.9in fire.

On 18 November 1914 the *Goeben* encountered the Russian Black Sea Fleet of 5 pre-dreadnoughts in fog about 20 miles off the Crimea. In an action of scarcely 10 minutes at 7000 — 8000yds the *Goeben* fired 19 — 11in APC and made 4 hits on the *Evstafi*, which had 33 killed and 35 wounded. She was hit once by her opponent, a 12in shell thought to be black powder filled and nose fused, holing the 6in armour of No 3 port 5.9in casemate, which detonated 3 — 5.9in HE shells, broke up 2 AP and as a result ignited the ready supply of 16 cartridges. The gun was put out of action, and gas, flames and smoke entered the magazine which served Nos 3 and 4 guns, but no ammunition ignited here. The casualties were 13 killed and 3 wounded.

On 26 December the *Goeben* struck 2 mines with charges of about 220lb laid in water nearly 600ft deep (the accepted limit was then 330ft) about 15 miles off the Bosphorus. The first mine exploded on the starboard side below the conning tower and the second on the port side just forward of the port wing barbette making respective holes of 540 and 670 sq ft. The torpedo bulkhead held with slight leakage from sprung rivets in the first case, while in the second it was bulged in to a maximum of 12in with damage to rivets and easily controlled leakage into the nearby 11in magazine and into the port aftermost boiler room where the 2 boilers were for a time out of use. About 2000 tons of water entered the ship, but there was no dock in Turkey where she could be repaired and cofferdams had to be used. Their construction and fitting took time and the port side hole was not repaired until 28 March 1915 and the starboard one until 1 May 1915. In the interim the *Goeben* put to sea more than once, particularly on 1 to 4 April when she covered a demonstration against Odessa. She was never engaged in the Dardanelles attack although if the

Wilhelmshaven and then in a floating dock at Hamburg where she was repaired by Blohm and Voss. She was ready for service on 30 July 1916.

On 24 April 1918 the *Moltke's* worst damage of the war occurred during the High Seas Fleet's abortive attempt to destroy the Norwegian convoy. The starboard inner screw fell off, the turbine raced and before the governor stopped the steam supply, the wheel of the engine turning gear disintegrated. Pieces of the wheel went through the auxiliary condenser outlet, several auxiliary steam pipes and into the main switchboard room. The latter and the starboard inner engine room filled from the auxiliary condenser, much water entered the starboard outer engine room, and salting of the boilers put all engines out of action. About 2000 tons of water flooded in and the *Moltke* was down by the stern. Eventually a diver succeeded in closing the sea valves on the auxiliary condenser so that the flooding could be overcome. The accident to the *Moltke* occurred at 06.10 and the dreadnought *Oldenburg* took her in tow at 11.50 after a previous attempt by the light cruiser *Strassburg* had failed. Apart from one break in the towing cable, a speed of 10-11kts was maintained. By 17.40 on 25 April the *Moltke's* engines were sufficiently in order for her to steam at 12-13kts, and about an hour later the tow was slipped off List. At 19.37 she was attacked by *E 42* about 40 miles to the north of Heliogland, and 1 — 18in torpedo hit in way of the port engine rooms. The total amount of water that flooded in, was as much as 1730 tons, but the *Moltke* was still able to steam, fired her 5.9in guns at the supposed position of *E 42* and made Wilhelmshaven at 3½-4kts without further incident. She was however under repair until the end of August.

The *Goeben* was the only German battlecruiser that did

British had entered the Sea of Marmora, the cofferdam would have been dropped and the *Goeben* used to defend the Bosphorus behind a minefield across the southern entrance. On 2 May 1915 she left for the Dardanelles to carry out indirect firing over the Gallipoli peninsula at British ships but the operation was cancelled.

On 10 May 1915 the *Goeben* was once more in action with the Black Sea Fleet, but on this occasion off the Bosphorus in good visibility. The *Evstafi*, *Ioann Zlatoust*, *Pantelimon* and *Trisvititelia* were present and for 22 minutes the *Goeben* engaged the *Evstafi* at 17 500 to 16 00yds but her shooting was not good on this occasion and Russian accounts say she made no hits, though it was thought in the *Goeben* that 3 had been seen. The Russian ships concentrated well and made 3 — 12in hits, one far forward on the forecastle which penetrated to the lower deck without very serious damage, one which burst on the lower edge of the belt sending up a water splash which put No 2 port 5.9in temporarily out of action, and one on the net casing so that the torpedo net hung down.

On 8 January 1916 she had her only action with one of the Russian dreadnoughts, the *Imperatritsa Ekaterina*, not the *Maria* as stated in the German Official History. The *Goeben* fired 5 salvos in the first 4 minutes but the range of 21 500 — 22 000yds was too great, and she retired towards the Bosphorus 75 miles away. The *Ekaterina's* 12 — 12in could, however, range to 28 300yds at 25°, and she continued to fire for 30 minutes, the final range being about 24 500 — 25 000yds. The Ekaterina expended about 150 — 12in shells but the *Goeben* was not hit except by numerous splinters. Though much the faster ship in good condition the *Goeben* with a very foul bottom and slack propeller shafts, had difficulty in escaping from the *Ekaterina* which is said in some accounts to have attained 23½kts.

By October 1916 there was such a shortage of coal that operations had to cease. In the summer of 1917 the *Goeben* was refitted and the inner shafts drawn, and her next operation was the sortie from the Dardanelles in company with *Breslau* on 20 January 1918. The *Goeben* struck a mine half an hour after leaving the Dardanelles, but she and the *Breslau* attacked Imbros, sinking the monitors *Raglan* and *M 28* and causing damage ashore. The *Goeben* appears to have fired 6 or 7 — 11in salvos in 6 minutes at about 10 000 — 7000yds at the monitors and another 7 salvos plus some 5.9in at targets in Kephalo Bay. The two ships then made for Mudros, but the *Breslau* and then the *Goeben* each struck a mine, and the former hit 4 more in succession and sank. The *Goeben* then entered the Dardanelles, striking a third mine on the way, and under unsuccessful bombing attacks from aircraft, but owing to confusing the buoy marking the gap in the anti-submarine nets with that marking Nagara Spit, ran hard aground at 15kts. The *Goeben* got off on 26 January with the aid of the old battleship *Torgut Reis* and 2 tugs, and proceeded to Constantinople.

Exact details of the *Goeben's* mine injuries are not to hand, but all were from British Elia mines with 220lb charges. The first exploded on the port side below the bridge without damaging the torpedo bulkhead, the second on the port side a little forward of the port wing barbette and thus in practically the same place as the second 1914 mine, and the third on the starboard side abreast the after engine room. The second mine bulged the torpedo bulkhead and several rivets flew out, but the boilers in the port after boiler room abreast of the explosion were undamaged, while the third mine also bulged the torpedo bulkhead, but less than the second, and the starboard LP turbines remained intact.

After the Germans occupied Sevastopol, the *Goeben* was docked there in June 1918 but little was done apart from scraping and coating the ship's bottom, and the port forward mine damage was repaired at Constantinople with use of a cofferdam from 7 August to 19 October 1918. The other two mine holes were not repaired until the 1926 — 30 overhaul.

Moltke
Drüppel

LION CLASS
LION, PRINCESS ROYAL

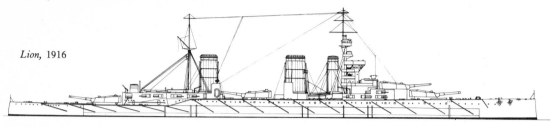

Lion, 1916

TABLE 10: **LION CLASS PARTICULARS**

Dimensions: 660ft (pp) 698ft (wl) 700ft (oa) x 88ft 6in x 28ft 0in mean.
Legend 26 350 ton (revised 26 475 tons).
Actual normal displacement: 26 270 tons at 27ft 8in mean draught.
Deep load: (less oil fuel):   29 680 tons at 30ft 7in mean (with oil 30 815 tons at 31ft 8in).
Sinkage: 98 tons/inch
Freeboard: 30ft forward, 25ft amidships, 19ft aft at legend draught.

	Builder	Machinery	Laid down	Launched	Completed
LION	Devonport	Vickers	29.9.1909	6.8.1910	.5.1912
PRINCESS ROYAL	Vickers	Vickers	2.5.1910	29.4.1911	.11.1912

DESIGN

These, the next two British battlecruisers, were a great improvement on the *Indefatigable* as indeed on 7600 tons greater legend displacement they could scarcely avoid being. Gun power and speed were well taken care of, but although their thickest armour was adequate against German 11in shells, there were large areas that were not, and none of the armour sufficed against German 12in. It may be noted that the *Lion* was the longest ship ever built in a Royal Dockyard.

ARMAMENT

The main armament of 8 — 13.5in/45 Mark V guns was in 4 twin turrets, arranged with a superfiring pair forward, one between the 2nd and 3rd funnels and one aft. Gun axis heights above legend waterline were 'A' 33ft, 'B' 42ft 6in, 'Q' 31ft 0in, 'X' 23ft 0in. A 5 turret distribution with 10 guns arranged as in the *Orion* class of battleship was considered and could have been accommodated in a 9ft longer hull than that actually adopted for the *Lion*. It was a pity in deciding on a 4 turret layout that the after superfiring turret and not the amidships one, was omitted. The 13.5in Mark V was an excellent gun of much improved accuracy over the 12in Mark X, and fired a 1250lb shell at a new gun 80°F muzzle velocity of 2593fs. The 13.5in BII mountings allowed 20° elevation which gave a range with the standard 4 crh shell of 24 000yds, but in 1914 neither sights nor range tables extended beyond 15° 21′ elevation and 20 500yds. When first completed there were only 2 hydraulic pumps to work the 4 turrets and a third pump was added to each ship in 1913. As usual in British ships of that period the magazines were above the shell rooms with their crowns formed by the armour deck except in 'Q' turret where it was one deck lower. The original peacetime outfit was 80 rounds per gun, 24 APC, 28 CPC, 28 HE and also 6 shrapnel, the war time outfit

being 110 per gun comprising 33 APC, 38 CPC and 39 HE. By Jutland this had been altered to 66 APC, 22 CPC, 22 HE, and after this battle it was recommended that the HE be reduced to 10 per gun, and then that the outfit should be 55 APC and 55 CPC. Finally it became 77 of the new APC and 33 CPC per gun. A main armament director was fitted on *Lion's* foremast by May 1915 and on Princess Royal by early 1916. A second main armament director was installed aft in *Lion* in September 1918 and in *Princess Royal* by the end of the year. By Jutland the sighting deficiencies had been corrected by fitting 'super elevation' 6° prisms to the director sights and centre position sights of turrets, so that the full elevation of the mountings could be used.

The secondary armament consisted of 16 — 4in 50 BL Mark VII in PIV* mountings in *Lion* and PII* in *Princess Royal*. These were arranged with 8 in the forward and 8 in the after superstructure, and the outfit was 150 rounds per gun, 45 CP and 105 HE, and later 38 CP, 90 HE and 22 HE Night Tracer. In April 1917 the number of 4in was reduced to 15 by the removal of the port aftermost gun from *Lion* and the starboard aftermost from *Princess Royal*. Secondary armament directors were approved in May 1918 but not fitted during the war. The 4 — 3pdr Hotchkiss saluting guns were reduced to 2 in April 1915 in *Princess Royal*, while *Lion* lost one overboard in a gale in 1914 and had another removed in August 1915. The number was again increased to 4 in both in May — June 1919.

The AA armament was complicated as usual. *Lion* had a 6pdr Hotchkiss fitted in October 1914 to which a 3in/20 cwt Mark I was added in January 1915. In July 1915 the 6pdr was replaced by a 2nd 3in, though for a time in 1916 — 1917 she appears to have had only one. In April 1917 she again had 2 — 3in/20 cwt Mark I which were retained till the end of her career. *Princess Royal* had a 6pdr Hotchkiss from October 1914 to December 1916, and a

3in/20 cwt Mark I from January 1915 to April 1917 when it was transferred to *Lion, Princess Royal* having in exchange the 2 — 4in BL VII, removed from her own and *Lion's* secondary armament, on 60° mountings. These were replaced in May 1919 by 2 — 3 in/20cwt Mark I and from June 1919 to March 1922 she also had 2 — 2pdr Mark II. The original outfits per gun were 500 HE for the 6pdr and 270 plus 30 shrapnel for the 3in, which was reduced to 120 HE and 30 incendiary, while the 4in had 75 nose fused common and 75 shrapnel and later 160 HE and 40 incendiary.

Torpedo-tubes and aircraft. There were 2 broadside submerged 21in TT forward of 'A' barbette and 14 torpedoes were carried and by the end of the war each ship had 2 Sopwith Camel's with flying off platforms on 'Q' and 'X' turrets.

ARMOUR

The belt armour extended to the upper deck and from the conning tower to the after end of the condenser rooms, it was 9in from the lower edge 3ft 6in below legend wl to the main deck and 6in between the main and upper decks. By 'B' barbette it was reduced to 6-5in, by 'A' and 'X' to 5in and forward and aft to 4in, ending in 4in bulkheads. The original design had included no forward 4in armour, the armour deck being relied on for protection. The barbettes of 28ft internal diameter were 9-8in above decks, 8in where behind the skin plating and 3in between the upper and armour decks except that 'X' was 4-3in, and 'Q' was further reduced to 1in below the main deck, at which level 'A' and 'B' were combined. The turrets had 9in faces and sides, 8in rears, 3½in roofs reduced to 2½in at the rear, and 3in exposed floors. After Jutland the roofs were increased to 4½-3½in. The funnel uptakes were 1-1½in between the upper and forecastle decks, and there were 1-¾in blast screens for 'Q' turret. The conning tower was 10in with 3in roof and 4in floor, but the after control tower only had 1in.

The armour deck was 1in from the forward 4in bulkhead to 'X' barbette, 1½in between 'X' and the after bulkhead and 2½in fore and aft beyond the bulkheads. It was at lower deck level, the centreline height above the keel varying by as much as 9½ft. The upper deck was 1in over the side armour, and the forecastle deck 1½-1¼in amidships. After Jutland 1in plating was added to the upper deck by the barbettes and also to the lower deck by 'B' and 'X' the total amounting to 130 tons. There were 2½-1½in longitudinal screens to 'A', 'B' and 'X' ammunition spaces, while 'Q' had a 2½in starboard screen near the side and a 1in port one well inboard.

By no stretch of the imagination can the above protection be considered in keeping with the main armament.

STABILITY

Calculated metracentric heights were 4.85ft at legend, 4.98ft at deep load and 5.83ft with oil, while actual figures were:
Lion 5.0ft, 5.0ft, 6.0ft and *Princess Royal* 4.95ft, 5.05ft, 5.95ft. September 1917 figures for the latter ship were 4.75ft, 4.82ft, 5.44ft.

MACHINERY

The 42 large tube Yarrow boilers, 235lb/sq in were distributed equally in 7 boiler rooms, the foremost on the centreline being 34ft long and the others to port and starboard 52ft. The aftermost pair were between 'Q' barbette and the engine rooms so that the forward group extended for 138ft. There were 2 sets of Parsons turbines with HP ahead and astern on the outer shafts and LP ahead and astern on the inner. These were arranged in 2 — 62ft long engine rooms and 2 — 50ft condenser rooms, the total floor area for the machinery being 6944 sq ft and for the boilers 12 590. Designed shp was 70 000 = 27kts and normal coal 1000 tons with max 3500 tons and 1135 tons oil fuel. This gave coal only/coal & oil radii of action of 1665/2420 sea miles at 24¼kts and 3395/4935 at 16¾kts.

On the Polperro mile *Lion* achieved 76 120 shp = 27.62kts at 279.2 rpm and *Princess Royal* 78 803 = 28.5kts at 284.8rpm. Both had propellers of the same design and as

usual were burning coal only, the different performance being attributed to a rough bottom coating in *Lion*. Subsequently on 8 July 1913, with different and apparently less satisfactory propellers, *Princess Royal* was worked up to 96 240 shp on the Polperro mile burning coal and oil but only achieved 28.06kts. She was 3 months out of dock and drawing 29ft 10in forward and 31ft 3in aft, so that the results were not comparable, but a higher speed had been hoped for.

GENERAL

When she first left Devonport *Lion* had a tripod mast abaft the fore funnel, a curious arrangement present in the *Dreadnought* and the *Colossus* and *Orion* classes, the only virtue of which was that the mast was a convenient support for the boat boom. The funnel smoke and gases could just be tolerated in the fore top in the battleships, but in the *Lion* steaming flat out with funnel gases at around 550°C it was an impossible and indeed ludicrous arrangement, though in point of fact the fore funnel served 10 boilers in *Lion* and 12 in the *Colossus* class. In February 1912 it was decided to replace the tripod by a pole mast forward of the fore funnel, which was later altered to a tripod by struts not reaching to the fore top. The 100 ton margin was taken up by armour additions, and the original legend exceeded by a further 125 tons (see Table 13).

The *Princess Royal* was sold for breaking up in December 1922 and the *Lion* in January 1924.

WAR SERVICE

Except when in dockyard hands the *Lion* was flagship of the battlecruisers throughout the 1914-1918 war.

In the the **Battle of the Dogger Bank** on 24 January 1915, the *Lion* expended 243 — 13.5in APC before she was put out of action, her targets being first the *Blücher*, then the *Derfflinger* and finally the *Seydlitz*. Only 4 hits were scored, one on each of the first two named and two on *Seydlitz*, one of which put the 2 after turrets out of action with a disastrous ammunition fire. The range was nearly always 16 000yds or more but *Lion's* shooting clearly left

much to be desired. She also expended 54 — 4in at German destroyers without success. The *Lion* was put out of action as a result of hits on her hull, the only occasion when the poor side armouring of the British battlecruisers was unequivocally demonstrated in battle, yet her casualties were only 1 killed and 20 wounded. Altogether she was hit by 16 — 11in or 12in shells (mostly 11in) and 1 — 8.3in of which all but one were from the port side. In chronological order these were:

1 17-18ft below lwl, one wing compartment flooded.

2 17-18ft below lwl, one wing compartment flooded.

3 8.3in from *Blücher* on 3½in 'A' turret roof. Roof dented and driven down a little. Left gun out of action for 2 hours.

4 11in from *Moltke* at about 18 000yds. Struck water about 15ft from side, ricochetted and pierced 5in armour aft, about 2ft above deep wl, making a hole 24in × 18in, then passed through escapes and vent trunks of 4in magazines, into which a piece of the shell dropped, through the ¼in main deck, was deflected upwards and finally dropped unexploded on the main deck. The after low power switchboard compartment was flooded, eventually causing 2 of the ship's 3 dynamos to be shorted.

5/6 2 — 11in hit together from *Seydlitz* at about 16 000yds. The shock was so great that it was at first thought *Lion* had been torpedoed — one shell struck 5in side armour forward, just below the main deck, drove in a piece 30in × 24in and burst 6ft from impact in a wing compartment abreast the torpedo body room, causing great damage in the latter. The torpedo body room flooded up to the main deck, the torpedo flat, the compartment below it, the port cable locker and the capstan compartment were also flooded. A splinter hole in the exhaust pipe from the capstan engine filled the auxiliary condenser with salt water and the resultant salting of the boilers eventually made it necessary to stop the starboard engine so that the *Lion* had to be towed home. (The port engine had previously been stopped as a result of hit No 16.) The other shell hit a little further aft, bursting on the 6in side

Princess Royal at full power trials on the Polperro Mile
CPL

armour 3-4ft below load wl. Two armour plates were forced in about 2ft, the outer and inner bottoms bulged in over an area of 40ft × 7ft, the slope of the 1in armour deck forced in and some of the foremost lower bunkers flooded.

7/8   2 — 11in hit together amidships at about 17000yds. One struck the 6in side just below the upper deck and burst 8ft inboard, while the other struck the junction of the 6in and 9in armour, at main deck level bursting 2ft inboard. Much damage was done to light structures.

9   11in went through the forecastle skin plating and the 1in upper deck bursting against the 8in armour of 'A' barbette. Little damage was done and a small fire in 'A' turret lobby was quickly put out.

The *Lion* was now dropping back and was overtaken by *Tiger.* Meanwhile 7 hits, Nos 10 to 16 occurred within 10 minutes or so at about 18000yds which cannot be given in chronological order:

10   Burst in bakery which was wrecked. Part of the shell passed through the armour gratings and holed the exhaust bend to the port inner condenser without damaging the tubes.

11   Hit 9in armour amidships, did not penetrate.

12   Through No 1 funnel and 1¼in forecastle deck, bursting 8ft beyond.

13   Through No 2 funnel and burst on skylight.

14   Through No 2 funnel and overboard.

15   Through forecastle deck and burst as it passed through ship's side.

16   Thought to be 12in from *Derfflinger.* Hit lower strake of 9in side armour abreast the engine room and just below the deep load wl and burst on the armour forcing a 16ft × 5ft 9in plate at least 2ft inward. The outer and inner bottom plating and the 1in armour deck slope were much torn and distorted. The port feed tank was opened to the sea, and overflowed into the reserve feed tank and thence into the port engine room, but the valves were shut and the port engine room saved from flooding. Luckily the discharge pipe from the air pumps to the feed tank held though badly distorted, as there was no stop valve here, and if the pipe had failed the engine room would have flooded. As it was the port engine had to be stopped and the feed suctions to the port boiler rooms closed. The feed tank bulkhead in the port engine room was badly bulged, 2 lower bunkers were flooded and the ship was heeling about 10° to port with speed reduced to 15kts. The rise in water level in the ship shorted the remaining dynamo, all light and power failed, and the *Lion* was now out of action.

17   On starboard side 17ft-18ft below lwl.

As all 3 of the German battlecruisers were frequently firing at *Lion* only a few hits can be assigned to individual ships. In addition to the above damage, the right gun of 'Q' turret was out of action after 15 rounds from incorrectly diagnosed trouble with the firing mechanism, and 4 minutes before *Lion* was overtaken by *Tiger,* 'A' magazine was erroneously reported on fire and flooded 2ft deep before it was found to be a false alarm.

The inadequacy of the *Lion's* 5in and 6in armour against 11in APC even at 20° to the plate normal was well demonstrated, and it may be noted that stronger supports behind armour joints and rounding off of sharp edges on the inner surfaces of armour plates to reduce their cutting action when displaced, were incorporated in the *Renown* and *Repulse* laid down on the day after the battle. The shallow water in which the action was fought, caused a steep wave profile at high speed, with its hollow amidships in wake of the machinery spaces thus giving a larger vulnerable area here than usual.

The *Lion* was temporarily repaired at Rosyth with timber and about 150 tons of very hard concrete, which took a fortnight to remove, largely by blasting when she was permanently repaired by Palmers, as it was not desired to admit that she was badly damaged enough to send to Portsmouth or Devonport. She was thus repaired on the Tyne, heeled 8° to starboard with 4 cofferdams, between 9 February and 28 March. About 1500 sq ft of outer bottom plating was damaged, and 20 armour plates had to be removed to repair the structure behind them. Five new armour plates were required.

The *Lion* was next in action at **Jutland** where her main target was the *Lützow,* though the *Derfflinger,* the *König* class and the light cruisers *Wiesbaden* and *Pillau* were also fired at. The ranges were mostly 14000 to 21000yds though at times 11000yds or less. Altogether the *Lion* expended 326 — 13.5in APC but can only be credited with 5 hits, 4 on *Lützow* and 1 on *Derfflinger* of which the latter and 2 on *Lützow* were at no more than 11000yds. She also fired 7 — 21in torpedoes—4 at the German battle fleet, 2 at *Derfflinger* and 1 at the disabled *Wiesbaden,* without success.

In return she was hit by 9 — 12in base fused HE from the *Lützow* coming from the portside, and by 4 — 12in from the *Lützow* and 1 — 5.9 in from starboard. There was only one really damaging hit, that on 'Q' turret by one of the above 9 from port. The range was about 16500 yds and the shell struck the right upper corner of the left gun port which was formed by the junction of the 9in centre face plate and the 3¼in roof. A piece of 9in armour was driven into the gunhouse and the shell also entered, was deflected slightly on the gun collars, and burst about 3ft from impact over the left gun. All in the gunhouse were killed or wounded, and the front roof plate and centre face plate blown off. A fire occurred in the gunhouse which the fire party thought they had extinguished from above. The magazine doors were closed and the magazine flooded. The position was now that a full 13.5in charge was in the right gun loading cage 4ft above the working chamber, in the left cage in the working chamber, in both waiting positions in the working chamber, in both lower hoist cages which were down, and in both magazine hoppers in the handing room, a total of 8 full charges. Twenty-eight minutes after the hit, the fire in the turret which had continued to smoulder, spread to the working chamber; it is not known how. Although venting was increased by part of the turret roof being off and the handing room hatch open, the 8 charges all of which were in authorised positions, ignited so violently that 'Q' magazine bulkheads were considerably buckled and bulged inwards though supported by the flooding water in the magazine. A venting plate admitted flame into the magazine but no harm was done. If the doors had not been closed, *Lion* would without doubt have blown up, and she very probably would have done so if the doors had been closed and the magazine not flooded, as the doors were by no means flash tight.

The other 8 hits from port in order from forward were:

1   Passed through forecastle deck and overboard without bursting.

2   Passed through a total of about 4½in of plating and caused a most troublesome fire in the Navigator's cabin on entry.

3   Burst on 1¼in forecastle deck at base of middle funnel, making a hole 12ft × 15ft in the casing. Two boiler rooms filled with fumes and smoke, while many fragments were caught by the armour gratings.

4   Ricochet, dropped unexploded near middle funnel.

5   Hit 6in upper belt and probably burst on impact.

6   Passed through roof and side of unarmoured after 4in control without bursting.

7/8   Two shells struck 5-6ft apart on ¼in plating between forecastle and upper decks abaft the after 4in battery. They passed through the starboard ¼in plating also, and burst just above or on the 1in upper deck 24ft from impact, making a hole 8ft × 8ft and causing many casualties among the 4in gun crews.

The 4,— 12in hits from starboard were:

1   Struck hull plating forward and burst on the port side.

2   Through mainmast without exploding.

3   Passed through after end of superstructure side and 1¼in forecastle deck, bursting 21ft from impact and causing much damage to light structure. Ready

Lion as altered soon after completion
CPL

Princess Royal, 1918/19
IWM

A rare view of *Lion* after Jutland with 'Q' turret removed
IWM

use 4in cordite on the forecastle deck was set on fire, and 2 — 4in guns in the starboard after battery disabled.

4 Pierced the 1in upper deck aft and burst 13ft away against the inside of the port 4in side armour. Smoke penetrating down caused a fire to be erroneously reported in 'X' port magazine which was partially flooded before the mistake was rectified.

The 1 — 5.9in burst on the upper part of an engine room uptake, causing a small fire.

Although the damage apart from that in 'Q' turret, was far less serious than at the Dogger Bank *Lion's* casualties were 99 killed and 51 wounded. The failure of the 2 master gyro-compasses which caused *Lion's* 360° turn was due to a nearby explosion, but all data on this has been destroyed, and it can only be said that it was not the immediate result of a hit. Other failures were that of the left chain rammer in 'A' turret, and the right main cordite cage in 'X' damaged in a mistaken attempt to double load the waiting position.

After the battle *Lion* was in the basin at Rosyth from 5 to 26 June, initially at 4 hours notice, and then at Armstrongs on the Tyne from 27 June to 8 July for 'Q' turret to be removed and her armour repaired. She was in No 1 dry dock at Rosyth from 8 to 20 July when her repairs were completed as a 3-turret ship, but 'Q' turret was not replaced till a further visit to Armstrongs from 6 to 23 September.

At the Dogger Bank battle *Princess Royal* was third ship in the line and at full speed dropied astern of *Lion* and *Tiger* perhaps due to unsatisfactory propellers or to fouling from her time in the West Indies. She fired 176 — 13.5in APC, 95 — 13.5in HE and also 2 — 13.5in shrapnel at the airship *L5*. Her targets were mainly the *Blücher* and *Derfflinger* but some rounds were fired at the destroyer *V5*. The total number of hits on the *Blücher* is not known but *Princess Royal* made 2, including the one that crippled her,

before she fell out of line, and 1 on the *Derfflinger*. No hits were made on *Princess Royal* in this battle.

At Jutland the *Princess Royal* was second ship in Beatty's line and flag of Rear-Admiral Brock commanding the 1st Battlecruiser Squadron. For a considerable part of the battle she was handicapped by smoke from the fires in *Lion* and only expended 230 — 13.5in mostly APC. Her target was chiefly the *Lützow*, though the *Derfflinger* and finally the *Seydlitz* and *Hannover* were also fired at, as well as the light cruisers *Regensburg* and *Wiesbaden*. She can be credited with 3 hits on *Lützow* and 2 on *Seydlitz*, the latter at under 10 000yds. The *Princess Royal* also fired 1 — 21in torpedo at the pre-dreadnoughts of the 2nd Squadron without success. Altogether she was hit by 6 — 12in shells coming from port and by 2 — 12in and 1 — 11in from starboard. The port hits were all from *Derfflinger* and in order from forward were:

1 Struck 6in belt and pierced the armour, bursting 5ft from impact, in a coal bunker although the range was about 15 500yds and the angle 25-30° to the normal. The shock of this hit and of No 3 put the Argo fire control tower temporarily out of action.

2 Went through a port cover 12ft aft of Hit 1 and burst 22ft from impact on the 1in upper deck. The 8in armour of 'B' barbette was slightly displaced by the explosion about 8ft away. Severe damage to light structure.

3 Burst or broke up on striking 6in upper belt.

4 Probably a ricochet. Burst on the junction of 6in and 9in side armour.

5 Passed through middle funnel without exploding.

6 Struck muzzle of 'Q' right gun and burst about 10ft away in the air. Slight damage to gun which continued firing.

The hits from starboard in similar order were:

1 11in from *Posen* nearly half severed starboard strut of foremast about 20ft above forecastle, passed through fore funnel and more than half severed port strut without exploding.

2 12in from *Markgraf* at about 13 000yds. Pierced 6in side armour, tore the main deck for 17ft, was deflected upwards, badly damaged the casings of both condenser rooms and burst 52ft from impact below the 1in upper deck in which a 6ft × 6ft hole was blown. Some 4in cordite was ignited on the main deck and both condenser rooms filled with dense smoke.

3 12in from *Markgraf* at same time as No 2. Hit 9in armour of 'X' barbette obliquely, glanced down through 1in upper deck and burst just below it. A large fragment of 9in armour was driven into the gunhouse and the turret jammed by the displacement and distortion of the 9in barbette armour. The burst caused considerable damage to light structure.

In addition to these hits the stud axis crank pinion sheared on the left gun of 'A' turret early in the battle and the breach could not be opened for 11 hours, while 'A' right gun suffered from misfires. The casualties in *Princess Royal* totalled 22 killed and 81 wounded. She was at Rosyth until 10 June when she went to Portsmouth and was repaired there from 13 June to 15 July, occupying No 14 Dry dock from 15 June to 10 July and arriving at Rosyth on 21 July.

QUEEN MARY

Queen Mary, 1916

TABLE 11: QUEEN MARY PARTICULARS

Dimensions: As *Lion* except 703ft 6in (oa) x 89ft.
Legend displacement: 27000 tons.
Actual normal displacement: 26770 tons at 27ft 7½in mean draught.
Deep load (less oil fuel): 30480 tons (31650 with oil at 31ft 8in)
Sinkage: 99 tons/inch.
Freeboard: as *Lion*.

	Builder	Machinery	Laid down	Launched	Completed
QUEEN MARY	Palmers	John Brown	6.3.1911	20.3.1912	.8.1913

DESIGN

This ship is often taken as one of the *Lion* class but in fact bore the same relationship to them as the *King George V* class to the *Orion's*. The Germans obtained details but it does not appear that these had the slightest influence on their designs.

ARMAMENT

The main armament was unchanged except that the 13.5in fired 1400lb shells with a new gun 80°F muzzle velocity of 2498 fs. The BII* mountings allowed 20° elevation at which the range was 23700yds though in 1914 sights stopped at 15°21 . Ammunition outfits were as in the *Lion* class. A main armament director was fitted on the foremast by December 1915 and 'super-elevation' 6° prisms to director and centre position turret sights by Jutland.

The secondary armament remained at 16 — 4in/50

BL Mark VII guns but they were in PVI mountings and the 8 guns in the forward superstructure were in an armoured battery at forecastle deck level, instead of being unarmoured on 2 deck levels. The original 4 — 3pdr Hotchkiss saluting guns were removed in early 1915, and in October 1914 1 — 3in/20 cwt Mark I and 1 — 6pdr Hotchkiss were added as AA guns. Ammunition outfits for all these were as in the *Lion* class, as was the torpedo armament.

ARMOUR

Protection was generally the same but there were some alterations. The 4in belt forward extended nearer to 'A' barbette, and the 5in lower strake was taken to about 7ft past the forward edge of 'B', while the after 4in belt did not extend as far along the main deck side as did the lower strake so that the after 4in bulkhead was in 2 steps. The funnel uptakes and 'Q' blast screens were mostly ¼in,

Queen Mary entering Devonport shortly after commissioning, 1913
CPL

oil to 3600 and 1170 tons. This gave radius of action figures (coal/coal + oil) of 1645/2390 sea miles at 24.9kts and 3415/4970 at 17.4kts. On the mile 28.17kts was achieved with 83 000 shp at 289 rpm on 2 June 1913.

GENERAL

As completed the *Queen Mary* had a pole foremast forward of the funnels, but it was later altered to a tripod with the struts not reaching the fore top. The 100 ton margin was used up in providing 1400lb 13.5in shells, the after control tower and a third hydraulic pump for the 13.5in mountings.

WAR SERVICE

The *Queen Mary* was in dock at Portsmouth when the Dogger Bank battle took place, and was blown up at **Jutland** 38 minutes after the battlecruiser duel began. For most of this time the *Queen Mary* which was the third ship was firing at *Seydlitz*, but latterly at *Derfflinger*. She is believed to have expended about 150 — 13.5in APC and made 4 hits on the *Seydlitz*. It is impossible to say exactly what happened when the *Queen Mary* was blown up, but it is thought she was hit by about 4 — 11in shells from the *Seydlitz* in the first half hour, including a hit in the after 4in battery, and perhaps another hit near 'X' turret. It is possible that there was considerable damage in the after 4in battery, including an ammunition fire noticed by the *Seydlitz*. About 5 minutes before she blew up a 12in from *Derfflinger* hit 'Q' turret on the sloping armour to the right of the right gun which was put completely out of action, though the left gun continued firing. This was followed by another 2 — 12in hits from *Derfflinger,* one of which was on 'A' or 'B' turret or barbette and the other perhaps on the left gun of 'Q' turret. An explosion somewhere in 'A' or 'B' shook the ship and hydraulic pressure failed in 'Q' turret according to the gauge. Immediately afterwards 'A' and 'B' magazines exploded, the forepart of the ship was broken off near the foremast and probably destroyed completely, while 'Q' and 'X' turrets were wrecked with a cordite fire in 'Q' working chamber. The after part of the ship was listing heavily to port, stern in air and propellers still revolving, and as the heel increased, a further explosion blew up the remains of the ship.

The shell that hit 'A' or 'B' was fired at 14 400yds, the angle of descent being about 12°. German 12in APC could pierce either the 9in turret face plate or the 9in barbette armour under these conditions, the face plate being easier as impact would be nearer to normal. Another easy path was through the $\frac{5}{8}$in or $\frac{3}{4}$in skin plating between the forecastle and upper decks, then the 1in upper deck and finally the 3in barbette base. Various other paths were possible, quite apart from a shell entering through one of the turret gun ports or hot fragments from a hit that failed to pierce, causing the disaster. 1266 were lost in the *Queen Mary.*

while the forward 4in gun battery was protected by 3in armour with 1in roof. The CT support was protected by 2in plating and the CT floor reduced to 3-2½in, an after control tower with 6in sides, 3in roof and 4in floor was added and the torpedo control tower was a 3in casting. The upper deck was thickened to 2in between 'A' and 'B' and the main deck was 1in over the lower strake of the after 4in belt. It is dubious whether these additions were worth the slight reduction in the side armour.

STABILITY

Calculated metacentric heights were 4.73ft at legend, 4.90ft at deep load and 5.7ft at deep load and oil, and actual figures 4.99ft, 5.08ft, 5.92ft.

MACHINERY

Boilers and engines were as in *Lion* but the designed shp was increased to 75 000 = 27.5kts and maximum coal and

TIGER

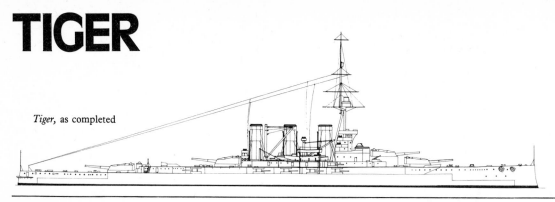

Tiger, as completed

TABLE 12: **TIGER PARTICULARS**

Dimensions: 660ft (pp) 698ft (wl) 704ft (oa) x 90ft 6in x 28ft 6in mean.
Legend displacement: 28 500 tons.
Actual normal displacement: 28 430 tons at 28ft 5in mean draught.
Extreme deep load: 35 710 tons with all fuel (but maximum wartime about 32 800 tons, carrying 3240 tons coal and 800 tons oil).
Sinkage: 101 tons/inch.
Freeboard: 30ft forward, 24½ft amidships, 19ft aft.

	Builder	Machinery	Laid down	Launched	Completed
TIGER	John Brown	John Brown	20.6.1912	15.12.1913	.10.1914

TABLE 13: **COMPARISON OF DESIGNED LEGEND WEIGHTS**

	LION class (revised weights)	QUEEN MARY	TIGER
Equipment (tons)	805 (3.0%)	805 (3.0%)	840 (2.95%)
Armament inc turret shields	3270 (12.3%)	3380 (12.5%)	3600 (12.65%)
Machinery and Engineer's stores	5340 (20.2%)	5460 (20.2%)	5900 (20.7%)
Coal (and oil, for *Tiger*)	1000 (3.8%)	1000 (3.7%)	900 (3.15%)
Armour and protection	6400 (24.2%)	6595 (24.5%)	7390 (25.9%)
Hull	9660 (36.5%)	9760 (36.1%)	9770 (34.3%)
TOTAL (tons)	26 475	27 000	28 400

It will be seen that in *Lion* some improvement in the percentage allotted to armour and protection was made over the *Indefatigable*, 23.7% as against 19.9%.

DESIGN

This, the last of the 13.5in battlecruisers, was in most ways except protection a distinct improvement on the 3 previous ships. It was decided to bring the boiler rooms together and site the amidships turret either between the boiler and engine rooms or else aft of the latter, in both cases forming a superfiring pair with the stern turret.

The original four designs were submitted on 14 August 1911, and 4 days later No 2 was approved. Further work on this design increased the legend to 28 200 tons and the shp to 82 000 (12 November 1911) and on 19 December 1911 it was approved to increase the shp to 85 000 = 28kts with extreme 108 000 =30kts. Meanwhile it had been decided to use all available spaces as oil tanks so that maximum fuel became 3340 tons coal and 3800 oil and the usual full load 2450 tons of each.

ARMAMENT

The distribution of **the main armament** was improved with the 4 twin 13.5in turrets arranged with a superfiring pair forward, one abaft the funnels with a clear field of fire aft and one further aft,·the two latter forming a widely separated superfiring pair. At legend draught gun axis heights were 33ft, 42ft 6in, 31ft 9in, 23ft, and otherwise the main armament was as in *Queen Mary*, the 8 — 13.5in Mark V guns firing 1400lb shells and the slightly modified BII** mountings allowing 20° elevation. War ammunition outfits were as in *Lion*. The *Tiger* completed with a main armament director at the fore top, the first battlecruiser to be so fitted, and as in the other 13.5in ships 'super-elevation' 6° prisms were installed by Jutland.

The secondary armament was completely changed and comprised 12 — 6in/45 Mark VII guns on PVIII mountings, 10 in a long upper deck armoured battery running from the foremast to abaft 'Q' barbette, and 2 in forecastle deck casemates just abaft the foremost battery guns. Of the latter 8 were located from the foremast to the after funnel and 2 aft of 'Q'. The ammunition outfit was 200 rounds per gun, 50 CP and 150 HE, later reduced to 120, to be made up of 30 CPC (Shellite filled), 72 HE and 18 HE Night tracer. As in most British ships with 6in batteries, the supply of ammunition to the guns was poor.

The forward 6in magazine and shell rooms were abaft those for 'A' and 'B' and one deck lower than the latter which were over the small arms and 3in AA magazines, while the after 6in ones were to port of those for 'Q', the 6in shell room in this instance being above the magazine. Two dredger hoists supplied ammunition passages from which there were individual hoists and hand-ups to the guns. At the Dogger Bank *Tiger* began the action with 20 rounds per gun in the passages and 20 more at each gun. German capital ships had combined 5.9in magazines and shell rooms each serving one or occasionally two guns, with individual dredger hoists and no ammunition passages. This ensured that a high rate of fire could be maintained and was also easier to make safe. Directors for the 6in guns were fitted to *Tiger* in 1917. The 4 — 3pdr Hotchkiss saluting guns were reduced to 2 in March 1915 and increased again to 4 in May 1919.

Unlike previous battlecruisers **the AA armament** remained at 2 — 3in/20 cwt Mark I from completion to November 1923. Originally 270 HE and 30 shrapnel were carried per gun, but this was reduced during the war to 120 HE and 30 incendiary.

The torpedo armament was increased to 4 submerged 21in TT, located to port and starboard forward of 'A' and aft of 'X'. 20 torpedoes were carried and it may be noted that *Tiger* successfully fired one while steaming at 29kts which exceeded by 2kts the 'record' made by *Princess Royal* and *Queen Mary*. By the end of the war *Tiger* carried a Sopwith Camel with flying-off platform on 'Q' turret.

ARMOUR

The armour belt was taken further forward and aft than in *Lion* but it was still at 9in from the conning tower to the after end of the condenser rooms only, and from 3ft 6in below legend wl to the main deck. It was reduced to 6in over this length between main and upper decks. Forward it was 5in to the upper deck from forward of 'A' to the CT, and likewise aft to the after edge of 'X'. Beyond these areas

it was 4in to the main deck, with a short extension to the upper deck forward of 'A'. A 2ft 6in wide strip of 3in armour was fitted below the belt from the forward edge of 'A' to the after edge of 'X'. The 4in belt ended in 4in bulkheads and there was an additional 4-2in bulkhead forward and a 4in one aft at the ends of the upper strake of the belt.

The battery armour took the side protection to 24ft 3in above lwl. It was 6in continued with 5in side armour and 5in angled bulkheads to 'A' and ending in a 4in straight bulkhead aft. There were 1in screens abaft the 2nd and 4th guns, and $\frac{3}{4}$in longitudinal rear screens with a 1½-1in roof. The two casemates had 6in faces, 2in rears and 1in roof. This was better side protection than in *Lion* but there was still only 5in by 3 of the 4 barbette bases, and in fact 'B' was worse off with 5in instead of 6-5in. The barbettes themselves were 9-8in above decks, 8in for one deck level on the exposed faces of 'A' and 'X' and 4-3in behind the 5in side armour, 'A' and 'B' being combined below the main deck. 'Q' differed in being 3in behind the 6in battery and belt and 1in behind the 9in belt. The turrets had 9in faces and sides, 8in rears, 3in exposed floors and 3¼-2½in roofs, increased to 4¼-3½in after Jutland. The conning tower had 10in with 4in floor and 3in roof, and 2in plating on the support, and the after control tower 6in with the same roof and floor as the CT.

The armour deck was 1in behind the side armour ending at the stern 4in bulkhead, but continued to the stem at 3in. The main deck was 1in over the belt ends and the upper deck 1½-1in over the rest of the belt, except where the 1½-1in forecastle deck covered the battery and 5in side armour extensions above the upper deck. After Jutland some parts of the armour, upper and forecastle decks were increased to 2, 2½ and 2½in respectively in wake of the barbettes, the weight added amounting to 179 tons. The screens to the ammunition spaces were 2½-1½in with less coal outboard of 'Q' and of the boiler rooms, than in the 3 other 13.5in battlecruisers.

1 Tiger at Rosyth, 1915

2 The canvas hangar and flying off platform added to *Tiger's* 'Q' turret late in 1917
IWM

STABILITY

Calculated metacentric heights were 4.9ft at legend and 6.3ft at extreme deep load, these figures having 0.7ft allowed off for the water free surface in the proposed anti-rolling tanks for which provision was made though they were not installed and deeper bilge keels fitted instead. The stability range was 74° at legend and 86° at extreme deep load with actual metacentric heights of 5.2ft and 6.7ft, while May 1918 calculations at 32800 tons gave 5.15ft.

MACHINERY

The machinery differed from that in the 3 previous ships. There were 5 boiler rooms each 35ft long, not divided to port and starboard, and in one group. The 39 Babcock and Wilcox 'large tube' boilers (235lb/sq in) were distributed with 7 in the foremost room and 8 in each of the others, and the 2 sets of Brown-Curtis turbines were in 2 engine and 2 condenser rooms, respectively 64ft and 46ft long. As usual the HP ahead and astern were on the wing shafts and the LP on the inner ones. As mentioned previously designed shp was 85000 = 28kts (275 rpm) and extreme 108000 = 30kts, while legend fuel was 450 tons each of coal and oil, and the 'normal' deep load figure 2450 tons each, though at one time it was 2800 tons coal and 2100 tons oil. The radius of action figures were not quoted in the usual detailed way, but 3270 miles at $24\frac{1}{4}$kts is given, apparently for 2450 tons coal plus 2450 tons oil.

Owing to the war full trials were not carried out, and on the mile at Polperro where there was hardly sufficient depth of water, 91103 shp gave 28.38kts at 267 rpm and 28990 tons, while 104635 shp = 29.07kts at 278 rpm and 28790 tons. These figures could doubtless have been improved with some development work on the propellers. At the Battle of the Dogger Bank where *Tiger's* displacement was probably at least 31500 tons, the greatest shp recorded was 96000 for 270 rpm and an estimated 28kts.

GENERAL

In appearance *Tiger* was quite distinct with 3 funnels equally spaced in one group, a tripod foremast with a high topmast, and only a derrick post for mainmast between the 2nd and 3rd funnels. With that rig she was by general consent one of the most handsome warships ever built, but in 1918 the fore topmast, previously reduced in height, was removed and the derrick post converted to a mainmast, alterations which according to the views of many, spoilt her appearance.

It will be seen that the figures in Table 13 show a general move in the right direction from those of the *Queen Mary* but little or nothing had been done to reduce machinery weights to reasonable levels. About 400 tons were added during the war of which the main items were 179 tons on decks and 77 tons on turret crowns.

The *Tiger* survived well into the post-war period and was not sold for scrapping until 7 March 1932. There were some changes in AA armament, the 2 — 3in being removed, and 4 — 4in QF Mark V were mounted in January 1924. These were reduced to 2 in November 1924, and in January 1925 replaced by 4 — 3in/20 cwt Mark I.

DESIGN 1:
27 250 tons legend 8-13.5in ('Q' between boiler and engine rooms), 16-4in. 76 000shp=28kts. 2700 tons coal, 1100 oil.

DESIGN 2:
28 100 tons 12-6in 79 000shp (otherwise as No. 1).

DESIGN 3:
28 100 tons legend 8-13.5in ('Q' aft of engine rooms) 12-6in 79 000shp=28kts. 3700 tons coal, 1100 oil.

DESIGN 4:
28 450 tons 16-4in 80 000shp (otherwise as No. 3).

TIGER APPEARANCE CHANGES
(Typical of modifications to later British battlecruisers)

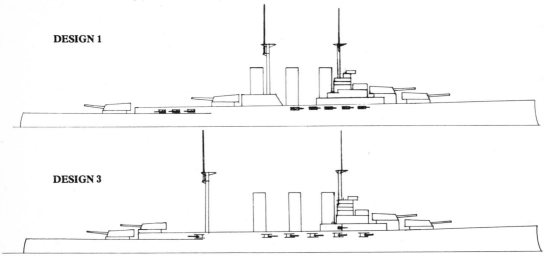

DESIGN 1

DESIGN 3

1 As designed, 1911

2 As completed, 1914

3 1915/1916

4 1917/1918

5 1918/1919

6 1924

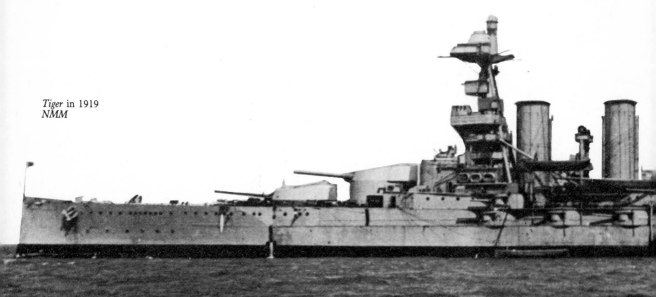

Tiger in 1919
NMM

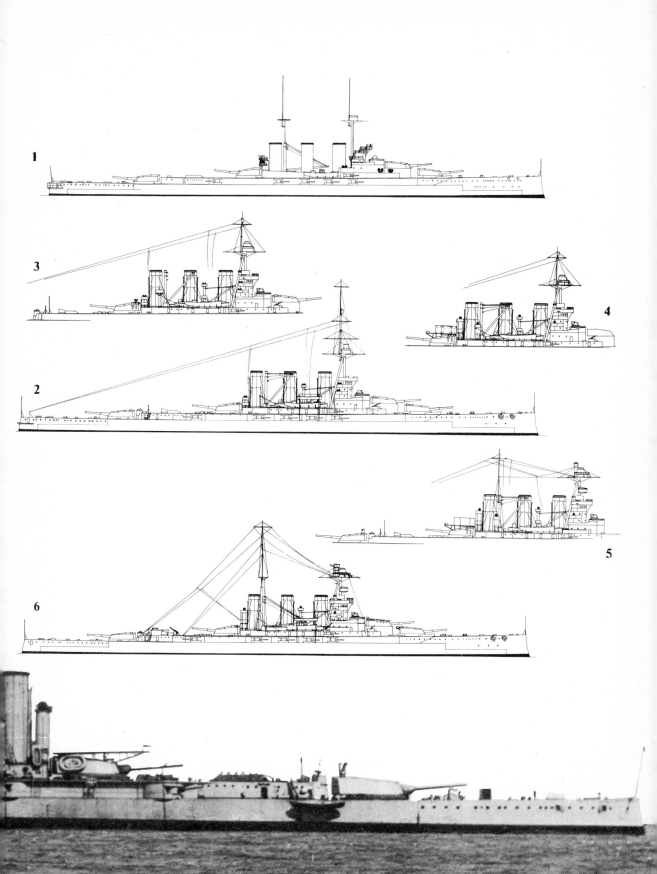

Finally in March 1929 the 3in were replaced by 4 — 4in QF Mark V. In addition 2 — 2pdr Mark II pom poms were carried from March to September 1928.

Her peacetime full load fuel was now 300 tons coal and 3300 oil, and 1927 figures indicate a speed of 25kts burning oil only and 28.1kts on coal and oil. If fully converted to burn oil only, speed would have increased to 28¼kts but that was postponed and never done.

WAR SERVICE

The *Tiger* was in action at Dogger Bank and Jutland, and was frequently and sometimes unjustly blamed for much of the disappointing performance of Beatty's battlecruisers. At the **Dogger Bank** where she was initially second ship in the line, *Tiger* expended 355 — 13.5in shells — 249 APC, 54 CPC, 52 HE — her targets being the *Blücher*, *Seydlitz* and *Derfflinger*, but not the *Moltke*, at which she should have been firing. It is not known how many hits were made on *Blücher* but *Tiger* scored one on each of her 2 battlecruiser targets. She also fired 268 — 6in HE. mostly at the *Blücher* with a few at German destroyers, and 2 — 21in torpedoes at the *Blücher*, one of which was thought to have hit though this is not probable.

The *Tiger* was hit by 6 heavy shells of which the first was before she overtook the *Lion*. This a 12in from *Derfflinger*, burst on the 9in belt. The other five hits were:
1 An 11in at about 17 500yds burst on the 3⅛in roof of 'Q' turret at the joint between 2 plates. Most of the shell was deflected overboard but fragments entered the turret, jammed the training gear and put the turret out of action with damage to the left gun breech mechanism.
2 Hit signal distributing office below the CT bursting 9ft from impact in the intelligence office. Very severe damage was caused to light structures and all communications between the control top and conning tower were destroyed. Above the burst the CT and the main and 6in gunnery control towers had 4in floors with access doors to all except the CT. These doors were open in the main and port 6in towers and all the occupants were casualties, while there were none in the CT and starboard 6in tower.

3 Hit 1½in forecastle deck amidships with severe damage to light structures.
4 Hit 9in belt below waterline with little damage.
5 On side armour forward. No details.

In addition to these an 8.3in went through the after funnel. *Tiger's* casualties were 10 killed and 11 wounded and her repairs were completed on 8 February.

At Jutland *Tiger* was fourth ship in Beatty's line until *Queen Mary* blew up and then third. She fired a total of 303 — 13.5in shells, mostly APC with some CPC, and made 3 hits, all in the first 35 minutes of which 1 was on *Moltke* and 2 on *von der Tann*. Apart from these ships she fired at *Seydlitz*, briefly at *Derfflinger* and also at the light cruisers *Regensburg*, *Wiesbaden* and apparently *Rostock*. In the final daylight action her targets included German dreadnoughts of the 1st Squadron, the old battleship *Hessen* and the light cruiser *Pillau*. Her 6in expenditure was 136 HE divided between the *Wiesbaden* and destroyers.

Altogether the *Tiger* was hit by 14 — 11in shells coming from port and 1 — 11in from starboard. The hits from port in order from forward to aft were:

1 Struck ⅛in forecastle deck about 107ft from bows and burst 22ft from impact with severe damage to light structures.
2 Shattered cable holder about 8ft abaft Hit No 1, passed through ⅛in forecastle deck and burst 8ft from impact. Severe damage to light structures.
3 Passed through scuttle about 14ft abaft Hit No 2, and burst 17ft inboard. Considerable damage to light structures near burst.
4 Passed through side plating and burst on 8 in armour of 'A' barbette. Plate driven in by up to 6in at lower edge. 'A' handing room severely affected by smoke and gas, but turret mounting uninjured.
5 Pierced 5in side armour and burst 4ft from impact.
6 Dented 5in side armour and deflected off.
7 Went through middle funnel. Possibly ricochet.
8 Passed through starboard side of ⅛in shelter deck, bursting 16ft from impact.

2

1 A rare view of *Tiger*, January 1915. Note bands painted on funnels and dark panel on hull amidships
CPL

2 The 'Pup' housed on 'Q' turret, 1917

3 *Tiger* in September, 1928
Wright & Logan

3

9 Burst on 3¼in front roof plate of 'Q' turret at about 13 500yds. The roof was holed over an area of 3ft 3in × 4ft 8in. Both gun loading cages were jammed but the left one could be used again after removing the cam rail actuating the cordite flash doors, though the right gun remained on secondary loading. The director gear was uninjured, and the guns were laid and trained by director and fired by percussion on hearing the forward guns fire. Three were killed and 5 wounded in the turret, and 'Q' only fired 32 rounds in the battle compared to 109 by 'B'.

10 Pierced 6in side armour a little below the upper deck and burst 22ft from impact and 8ft from the after 6in hoist. 2 — 6in charges near the top of the hoist were set on fire but the flash did not pass down the hoist. Severe damage was done to light structures, whilst the base of the shell went through the 1in armour deck and penetrated the ¾in thick web of the main steam pipe, and the armour deck was also holed by another fragment. The after 6in magazine was flooded and due to faults in a ventilation pipe valve and in venting plates 'Q' port magazine and the after 6in shell room flooded, and water also entered 'Q' shell room.

11 Struck 6in side armour. Plate forced in 3in maximum.

12 Struck 9in side armour. Plate forced in by 4in maximum.

13 Hit 'X' barbette at about 13 500yds on 9in armour near junction with 3in armour and 1in upper deck. A piece of 9in armour 27in × 16in was broken off, and the shell entered the turret through the revolving structure about 3ft below the turret shield, but did not explode properly though the filling ignited. The centre training shaft was smashed, one of the flash doors jammed, the left gun depression control valve casting fractured and director laying and firing circuits cut. After 7 minutes the turret began firing again with both guns in director training, individual laying and percussion firing. A total of 75 rounds was fired by 'X' in the battle but some probably went very wide as 2 hours 17 minutes after the hit it was discovered that the turret was 19° off its correct bearing in director training.

14 Ricochet struck 4in side aft. A wing compartment was flooded above the armour deck.

Of the above 14 hits No 3 was from *Seydlitz* and the rest from *Moltke*. The 3 bad hits Nos 9, 10 and 13 all occurred in the first 7 minutes of the battle as did Nos 2, 4 and 8 with Nos 5, 6 and 14 a few minutes later.

The one hit from starboard came from *Seydlitz* and was possibly a ricochet, passing through the after funnel.

There were also 3 — 5.9in hits on the side plating, 2 from port and 1 from starboard, the *Tiger* being the only British capital ship on which such hits are recorded in full.

In addition to the above damage the right gun of 'A' was put out of action after firing 27 rounds by a fracture in the valve box and control plunger of the run-out cut-off valve, and temporary repairs were not completed till after the action was over. Casualties in *Tiger* totalled 24 killed and 46 wounded. She was repaired in No 2 dry dock at Rosyth from 3 June to 1 July 1916 and was ready on the following day, the first of the 13.5in battlecruisers to complete repairs.

Battlecruisers at Scapa Flow, 1918. The battleship *Agincourt* is also visible, second from right
IWM

SEYDLITZ

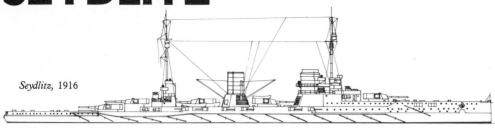

Seydlitz, 1916

TABLE 14: **SEYDLITZ PARTICULARS**

Dimensions: 656ft 2in (wl) 657ft 11in (oa) x 93ft 6in x 26ft 11in mean.
Legend displacement: 24 594 tons (usual fighting trim was about 30ft 6in forward, 30ft aft, at around 28 100 tons).

	Builder	Machinery	Laid down	Launched	Commissioned for trials
SEYDLITZ	Blohm & Voss	Blohm & Voss	4.2.1911	30.3.1912	22.5.1913 **completed** 17.8.1913)

DESIGN

This, the first of the next generation of German battlecruisers, was essentially a more heavily armoured *Moltke* and it might well be thought that 12in guns should have been introduced. Her design was worked out from March 1909 to January 1910, and she was built under the 1910-11 programme by Blohm and Voss who were also responsible for the machinery. Details of her design were obtained by the British but these appear to have no influence whatsoever on future ships. The *Seydlitz's* proportions differed from those of the *Moltke* and there was an additional weather deck extending from the stem to the foremast.

ARMAMENT

The main armament of 10 — 11in SKL/50 in 5 twin turrets was arranged as in *Moltke* with training arcs of 300° for the fore turret, 290° for the after pair, 180° on the near beam and 125° on the far beam for the wing turrets. Gun axis heights above lwl were: fore turret 34ft 1in, wing turrets 26ft 10in, after turrets 27ft 8in and 19ft 9in. It will be noted that except for the fore turret on the additional weather deck, the heights were slightly less than in *Moltke*. The 11in mountings were Drh LC/1910 resembling those in *Moltke,* and initially giving $13\frac{1}{2}°$ elevation increased to 16° before Jutland. In all turrets the shell rooms were below the magazines and on the platform deck or a flat above this. The ammunition outfit was 87 APC per gun though British Intelligence figures give 96 for the centreline and 81 for the wing guns. Director pointers for main and 5.9in guns were fitted in 1915.

The 12 — 5.9in SKL/45 guns in MPLC/1906 mountings were in an upper deck battery, extending from the fore funnel to just forward of the main mast, and 160 rounds per gun were carried. Originally there were also 12 — 3.45in SKL/45 in MPLC/1906 mountings with 250 rounds per gun. Of these 4 were forward below the weather deck, 2 in the forward superstructure, 4 aft of the 5.9in battery and 2 in shields on the after superstructure. These last were replaced early in the war by 2 — 3.45in Flak L/45 in 70° MPLC/1913 mountings, and by Jutland the others

had also been removed. There were 4 submerged 20in TT (1 bow, 1 stern, 2 broadside forward) and 11 torpedoes were carried.

ARMOUR

The armour belt was 12in between end barbettes from 4ft 7in above to 1ft 2in below lwl and tapered to 6in at 5ft 7in below lwl. From the upper edge of this belt to the upper deck the side armour tapered from 12in to 9in, with a further taper to 8in at the lower edge of the battery gunports. The belt and side armour was continued forward for the same height and depth at $4\frac{3}{4}$in for 59ft and then at 4in to the stem and also aft as high as the main deck ports and to within 10ft of the stern, at 4in. The battery armour was 6in above the lower edge of the ports, with 0.8in rear bulkheads and screens between the guns, and ended in 6in bulkheads while the bulkheads at the ends of the main side armour were $8\frac{3}{4}$-8in and the stern bulkhead 4in.

The barbettes were 9in above the side armour except that the forward and the after superfiring ones were reduced to 8in where screened by the CT and aftermost barbette respectively. The outer faces of the forward and aftermost barbettes were taken to the armour deck at 9in, but elsewhere the centreline barbettes were drastically reduced to 1.2in behind the 9-12in side armour. The 2 wing barbettes were reduced to 4in behind the battery armour and to 1.2in behind the 9-12in side, while the turrets had 10in faces, 8in sides, $8\frac{1}{4}$in rears, 4in sloping front roofs, $2\frac{3}{4}$in flat roofs and 4-2in floors. The fore CT had 14-10in armour with 3.2in roof, and the after CT 8in with 2in roof.

The armour deck was 1.2in amidships with the flat part 4ft 7in above lwl, forward it was 2in and 3ft 11in below lwl and aft 3.2in at 6in below lwl with 2in slopes. The upper deck was 1in outside the battery area, and the forecastle deck where it formed the battery roof 2.2in over the guns, 1.4in by the wing barbettes, and 1in inboard. Underwater protection was as usual in German ships with the torpedo bulkhead between end barbettes. It was 13ft 2in inboard amidships and 1.2in thick increased to 2in by ammunition spaces and ending in 0.8in transverse bulkheads. Above the armour deck the torpedo bulkhead was continued as a 1.2in splinter bulkhead to the upper deck.

STABILITY
Metacentric height is given as 10.23ft, the greatest of any First World War German capital ship, and Frahm anti-rolling tanks were fitted though not so used.

MACHINERY
The 5 main boiler compartments were each divided into 3 by longitudinal bulkheads giving a total of 15 boiler rooms, the foremost 3 having 1 boiler each and the others 2. The 27 Navy type Schulz-Thornycroft boilers worked at 235lb/sq in and there were 2 sets of Parsons type turbines with 4 shafts. The HP turbines were in the 2 forward engine rooms on the wing shafts, and the LP in the 2 after engine rooms on the inner shafts, with 2 auxiliary engine rooms inboard of the forward main ones. The nominal designed shp was 63 000 = 26.5kts, and on the mile 89 740 = 28.13kts was obtained at 329 rpm. Legend coal was 984 tons and maximum 3540 to which about 200 tons tar oil was later added, and the radius of action 2280 sea miles at 23.7kts and 4020 at 16.2kts.

The areas occupied by the machinery and boilers were respectively 4347 and 9960 sq ft compared with 6944 and 12 590 in *Princess Royal*, and the engine rooms would have been considered cramped by British ideas. Tandem rudders were fitted of which the forward one was somewhat ineffectual as in *Moltke* and like all German battlecruisers *Seydlitz* turned slowly and with considerable loss of speed.

GENERAL
The stem was nearly straight with a sharp rise of floor forward and in general appearance *Seydlitz* was similar to *Moltke* except for the extra deck forward. Pole masts were retained throughout her career. She was far better protected than her contemporary *Queen Mary* except perhaps for the main armament and this was also outweighted by the latter's 8 — 13.5in. The *Seydlitz* was scuttled with the rest of the German fleet at Scapa on 21 June 1919 and was salved for scrap in November 1928.

WAR SERVICE
During the 1914-18 War *Seydlitz* was usually flagship of the battlecruisers (1st Scouting Group) until *Hindenburg* entered service, though *Lützow* was flagship at Jutland

In the Dogger Bank battle on 24 January 1915 *Seydlitz* fired at *Lion* and finally at *Tiger* after the former had dropped out. She expended about 390 — 11in APC and probably made at least 8 of the 22 hits obtained. A total of 3 hits were made on her. The first from *Tiger* was forward and apparently did no very great damage, while the third from *Lion* at about 16 500yds burst on the 12in belt amidships with little effect. The second hit from *Lion* at about 17 000yds caused much destruction. This shell struck the quarterdeck and burst in holing the 9in barbette armour of the sternmost turret. The shell was kept out but armour fragments entered, piercing the ring bulkhead, and ignited 11in main and fore charges in the working chamder. The flash ignited the charges in the gunhouse, and those in the lower hoists and handing room, as well as some in the magazine also caught fire. The ignition of

these charges was at first comparatively slow, as when the fumes of the burning charges in the working chamber began to penetrate to the handing room one deck below, the crew of the latter opened the bulkhead door leading to the handing room of the after superfiring turret to escape. At this moment the charges in the handing room ignited and flash passed into the superfiring turret, setting fire to charges in the handing room and to some in the magazine and also in the working chamber and gunhouse. Altogether 62 complete (main and fore) charges were destroyed totalling over 6 tons of propellant. Fumes and flames penetrated through the damaged ventilation system and made the after part of the ship untenable, but it was possible to flood the magazines and the stern torpedo flat before the 11in shells started exploding from the heat of the fire. The flooding water spread to other compartments through damaged ventilation trunks and the draught aft rose to about 34½ft, while the steering compartments had to be abandoned for half an hour from fumes. Altogether *Seydlitz's* casualties were 159 killed and 33 wounded; it is obvious that far too many charges were present between magazines and guns. The *Seydlitz* entered the Wilmhelmshaven floating dock on the night of the battle, and was ready again on 1 April 1915.

On 24 April 1916 on the way to raid Lowestoft the *Seydlitz* struck a British Service mine (300lb wet gun-cotton charge) which exploded on the starboard side 13ft below lwl and just abaft the broadside TT. This was forward of the torpedo bulkhead, and the skin plating and the 2 nearest longitudinal bulkheads were destroyed or damaged for a length of 50ft, while there was some leakage in the transverse bulkhead joining the torpedo bulkheads. A torpedo warhead was badly damaged, but as in *Moltke* the explosive filling remained inert. The *Seydlitz's* draught forward increased by 4¼ft and 1400 tons of water flooded in but she was able to return to Wilhelmshaven at 15kts. She was reported ready on 22 May 1916 but a flooding test on 23/24 May showed that the broadside torpedo flat was not watertight and another 5 days' work was necessary. This was one of the factors that delayed the operation which led to the Battle of Jutland on 31 May/1 June 1916.

At Jutland *Seydlitz* was third ship in the 1st Scouting Group and initially engaged *Queen Mary* and then *Tiger*. Her later targets cannot always be identified but included *Warspite* and *Colossus*. Altogether she fired 376 — 11in APC and is believed to have made 10 hits: 4 on *Queen Mary*, 2 on *Tiger*, 2 on *Warspite*, 2 on *Colossus*. In the first 80 minutes *Seydlitz* fired about 300 — 11in and only made the 6 hits on the battlecruisers, while she made 4 hits of which the 2 on *Warspite* were at long range, from about 76 — 11in during the rest of the battle. *Seydlitz* also fired 450 — 5.9in, the most of any German ship, at destroyers, battlecruisers and *Defence*.

Altogether *Seydlitz* was hit by 22 heavy shells and 1 — 21in torpedo. In chonological order these were:

'Run to South'
1   13.5in from *Queen Mary* — holed side plating forward of foremast and burst over 1in upper deck in which a 10ft x 10ft hole was made. Great damage to light structures and partly as a result of this hit, subsequent flooding spread to the main deck near 'A' barbette and thence to 'A' magazines and the ship's control room.

Seydlitz
Drüppel

2 13.5in from *Queen Mary* — struck 9in armour of after superfiring barbette at 14 500 — 15 000yds and burst in holing. Fragments of armour and shell splinters holed ring bukhead, and 2 main and 2 fore charges in working chamber ignited. The turret training (which had already failed) and elevating gear and hoists were put out of action.

3 13.5in from *Queen Mary* burst underwater near skin plating amidships and wings flooded for 36ft.

4 13.5in from *Queen Mary* struck hull plating at about 18 000yds and then joint between 8-9in port sill plate and 6in battery after bulkhead. Burst in holing, and much damage caused, shell fragments travelling across the ship. No 6 starboard 5.9in gun out of action.

5 15in from 5th Battle Squadron. Went through forward weather deck and burst, holing weather deck, forecastle, and upper decks.

Torpedo hit from *Petard* or possibly *Turbulent*. Hit starboard side in line with the forward part of 'A' barbette, holing the skin plating for about 40ft x 13ft and flooding the wings for 91ft (and later for a further 20ft) and the outer and protective bunkers for 83ft. The torpedo bulkhead, here 2in, held though leaking considerably at its junction with the armour deck, and the water column from the explosion lifted the muzzle of No 1 5.9in and jammed

the gun so firmly that it was out of action. For the moment *Seydlitz* could maintain full speed, but eventually the whole 64ft section between the forward citadel bulkhead and the foremost boiler room bulkhead filled up to the armour deck.

'Run to the North'

6 15in from *Barham* or *Valiant* — went through weather deck 65-70ft from the bows, and burst 6ft from the starboard side above the forecastle deck, tearing a hole about 10ft x 13ft in the skin plating between the weather and upper decks and one about 6ft x 6ft in the forecastle deck while fragments holed the upper deck. This large hole in the starboard skin plating was the chief cause of *Seydlitz's* subsequent flooding troubles. Large amounts of water poured in at speed and aided by damage from 4 other 15in hits, gradually spread to all forward compartments above the armour deck. As the forecastle continued to sink deeper, water was able to enter aft of the citadel bulkhead through damage in that part of the ship, and also gradually penetrated to forward compartments below the armour deck through leakage at cable joints, voice pipes, ventilation trunks and hatches.

7 15in from *Barham* or *Valiant* — went through weather deck on port side about 20ft aft of No 6 and

Seydlitz at Wilhelmshaven after Jutland. The enormous damage
is apparent
Drüppel

burst immediately, blowing a hole 6ft x 6ft in the weather deck and one 20ft x 23ft in forecastle deck.

8 15in from *Barham* or *Valiant* — burst in holing 10in face of starboard wing turret at about 19 000yds. Effect mostly outwards but armour fragments and 2 pieces of shell entered wrecking the right gun elevating gear, but it could be moved by coupling to the left gun.

9 15in from *Barham* or *Valiant* — burst under water in line with foremast.

10 15in APC from *Barham* or *Valiant* — pierced upper edge of 4¾in side armour and burst against the capstan drum, tearing holes about 16ft x 23ft in upper and main decks.

11 15in from *Barham* or *Valiant* — possibly before No 10 — struck port windlass drum and burst, blowing holes in weather and forecastle decks.

First Fleet Action

12 Probably 12in APC from *Indomitable* — struck obliquely on 12in belt aft. *Seydlitz* severely shaken so that coupling at the upper steering engine flew out and ship had to be steered temporarily from steering gear compartment.

Second Fleet Action

13 12in HE from *Hercules* — went through after upper SL platform and burst near ship.

14 12in HE from *Hercules* — possibly before No 13 — burst on net boom amidships. Upper belt armour undamaged but torpedo net fittings destroyed over a large area and skin plating bulged in below belt, flooding wings for 40ft.

15 12in APC from *St Vincent* — probably richochet, went through skin plating and forecastle deck at waterway abreast bridge, exploding on entry.

16 12in APC from *St Vincent* — burst in holing 8¼in rear armour of after superfiring turret disabled by Hit No 2. Most of the explosive effect was inside the turret, and 2 main and 2 fore charges still laying in the cartridge loading

trays were ignited, and much other damage caused. Splinters deflected down outside the turret holed the 1in upper deck and cut the cables for the main training gear of the aftermost turret.

17 15in from *Royal Oak* — struck right gun of port wing turret. Gun badly dented and flattened, and turret director-pointer gear disabled. The shell burst and splinters put No 5 port 5.9in gun out of action.

Last Daylight Action

18 13.5in from *Princess Royal* — burst in holing 6in armour of No 4 port 5.9in casemate. Explosive effect inside casemate. Gun disabled and one ready cartridge burnt. Fragments of armour and splinters wrecked most of the port 5.9in fire control cables and cut those to the main wireless transmitter.

19 13.5in from *Princess Royal* — burst near CT above bridge.

20 12in from *New Zealand* — struck 2¼in roof of aftermost turret, deflected and burst about 3ft away.

21 12in from *New Zealand* — struck 12in belt near plate edge and broke up or burst. Armour holed but not displaced. An outer bunker flooded for 35ft. Range about 9500yds.

22 12in from *New Zealand*, possibly before No 21 — struck 12in upper belt just above junction with main belt and burst after penetrating a small distance. Armour holed and slightly displaced.

Earlier in the battle *Seydlitz* was also hit by 1 — 4in and 1 — 6in or 5.5in, both on the side armour with negligable effect. Apart from hits, a back-flash in the forward turret passed down the shell hoists to the working chamber, and a pencilled note in her report says that the force of this was a new experience. There were however no fatalities and apparently little if any damage. Altogether *Seydlitz's* casulties were 98 killed and 55 wounded.

At dusk (2100 GMT) on 31 May, *Seydlitz* had a calculated 2636 tons water on board with an increase in

Seydlitz down by the bow is assisted into Wilhelmshaven after Jutland (also overleaf)
Drüppel

48

draught forward of 8ft 4in, a decrease of 3ft 3in aft and a list of 2° 5′ to starboard. This was in itself no very serious danger to the ship, but the large hole in the starboard side forward from Hit No 6 was not far above the then waterline. Instead of joining *Derfflinger* and *von der Tann* at the rear of the German line, *Seydlitz* followed *Moltke* at revolutions for 22kts towards the van. Speed was later reduced to revolutions for 20-21kts, which gave perhaps 18-19 over the ground, but this was still much too high. Horns Reef Lightship was passed at 0400 on 1 June and *Seydlitz* once again joined the fleet at 0540, having lost touch during the night. It was now no longer possible to maintain the fleet speed of 15kts and *Seydlitz* reduced to 10 and then 7kts. Piloted by the *Pillau* and eventually going astern at 3-5kts with the pumping steamer *Boreas* draining the port forward casemates, *Seydlitz* was only got back to

Wilhelmshaven with great difficulty, anchoring inside the boom at 0325 on 3 June. Her condition was probably at its worst at 1700 on 1 June, a calculated 5329 tons of flood water giving a draught of 46ft 1in forward and 24ft 4in aft with an actual list of 8° to port.

While at anchor the guns and some of the armour of 'A' turret were removed, but strong currents interfered with patching, and at high water on 6 June *Seydlitz* entered stern first the South Lock which had a depth at MHWS of 45ft at the outer sill and 36ft at the inner. Here temporary repairs made rapid progress, the port wing turret guns were removed and on 13 June *Seydlitz* was towed out of the lock with a max draught of 34ft 3in, and entered the floating dock for permanent repairs which were completed on 16 September 1916.

DERFFLINGER CLASS
DERFFLINGER, LUTZOW

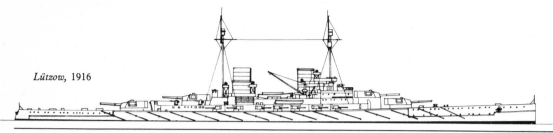

Lützow, 1916

TABLE 15: **DERFFLINGER CLASS PARTICULARS**

Dimensions: 686ft (wl) 690ft 3in (oa) x 95ft 1¾in x 27ft 2in mean.
Legend displacement: 26 180 tons (*Lützow* 26 318).
Deep load: About 30 700 tons at 31ft mean draught (fighting draught at Jutland 30ft 8in for *Derfflinger*)
Freeboard: 24ft forward, 15ft aft.

	Builder	Machinery	Laid down	Launched	Comissioned for trials
DERFFLINGER	Blohm & Voss	Blohm & Voss	.1.1912	1.7.1913	1.9.1914
LÜTZOW	Schichau, Danzig	Schichau, Danzig	.5.1912	29.11.1913	8.8.1915

DESIGN

These two ships were a great improvement on *Seydlitz* from which they differed markedly in general design. Together with their half-sister *Hindenburg* described later, they were generally and rightly considered the best battlecruisers to be completed up to the end of the First World War.

Derfflinger completed in November 1914, but there was serious turbine trouble during *Lützow's* trials, and she did not join the 1st Scouting Group until the end of March 1916. According to her gunnery officer, Commander Paschen her turret guns were not fired with full charges until the Lowestoft raid of 25 April 1916, and though at Jutland 5 weeks later her gunnery was of the highest quality, her water-tight integrity was far below the usual good German standards.

ARMAMENT

The main armament was much improved and comprised 8 — 12in SKL/50 guns firing an 893lb shell at 2835fs (80°F charge temperature) in 4 twin turrets, arranged in superfiring pairs forward and aft, the latter pair being separated by the length of the after engine rooms. The mountings were Drh LC/1912 allowing 13½° elevation, increased after Jutland to 16° in *Derfflinger*, respective ranges being 20 450 and 22 300yds. Arcs of training were 300° for the forward and 310° for the after guns, and gun axis heights at legend wl 'A' 26ft 11in, 'B' 35ft 7in, 'X' 30ft 4in, 'Y' 20ft 9in. For 'A', 'B' and 'X', magazines were on the platform and shell rooms on the lower deck, but for reasons of space this was reversed in 'Y' turret, and this turret also differed in that the shell hoists were not broken at the working chamber. The outfit was 65 APC and 25 base fuzed HE (really uncapped SAP) per gun. Director-pointers were fitted to *Derfflinger* in 1915 for 12in and 5.9in guns, and *Lützow* completed with them, while the latter had an experimental pattern of Petravic

gyro sight gear for the 12in at Jutland, though it was not used, and a later pattern was subsequently fitted to *Derfflinger*.

The secondary armament was originally to have been 14 — 5.9in SKL/45 guns in an amidships upper deck battery and this was retained in *Lützow*, but the No 4 port and starboard guns were replaced in *Derfflinger* while building by anti-rolling tanks, so that she had 12 — 5.9in. The mountings were MPLC/1906, II and outfit 160 rounds/gun. *Derfflinger* completed with 4 of the original 12 — 3.45in SKL/45 guns in MPLC/1906 mountings in the forward superstructure, but these were later removed and both ships had 8 — 3.45in Flak/45 guns in 70° MPLC/1913 mountings at Jutland, 4 by the fore funnel and 4 by 'X' turret, the latter 4 being subsequently removed in *Derfflinger*. There were 4 submerged TT(1 bow, 1 stern, 2 broadside forward of 'A') and 12 torpedoes were carried, 20in in *Derfflinger*, but 23.6in in *Lützow*, the first ship to have this size.

ARMOUR

The main belt ran from 'A' barbette to a little past 'Y' and was 12in from 4ft 7in above to 1ft 2in below lwl, tapering to 6in at the lower edge 5ft 7in below lwl and to 9in at the upper deck. Many of the plates were large and extended over the full depth of the side armour. Forward and aft the side armour reached to the main deck ports, except near the bows where it was taken to the upper main deck. It extended to the stem, but stopped about 15ft from the stern ending in a 4in bulkhead. Forward it was 4¾in reduced to 4in for most of its length and aft 4in. The main belt bulkheads were 10-8in, and the battery 6in with 0.8in screens and rears, and angled 6in bulkheads to 'B' and 'X'.

The barbettes were 10¼in, 'B' and 'X' being reduced to 4in where behind the battery armour, and all to 2.4in behind the main side armour, with a further reduction to 1.2in for 'A' and 'B' below the upper main deck. The forward face of 'A' was taken to the armour deck at 10½in. The barbette clear internal diameter was 27ft 11in and the ball track diameter 24ft 0in. The turrets had 10¾in faces and rears, 8¾in sides, 4.3in front roof plates sloping at about 15°, 3.2in flat roofs, 2in floors and 1in splinter bulkheads between the guns. The forward CT had 14-12in with 5-3.2in roof and 8-6in base, the 14in armour being as usual limited to a portion of the curved front of the raised after part which formed the gunnery control tower, and the after CT had 8in with 2in roof.

The armour deck was 1.2in amidships, 2in forward and 3.2-2in aft and the upper deck 1.2-0.8in where not covered by the battery roof which was 2-1.2in over the casemates and 1in inboard of them. The torpedo protection was on the usual German lines for the length of the main belt, the torpedo bulkhead being 1.8in with 1.2in bulkheads athwartships at the ends, and continued as a 1.2in longitudinal splinter bulkhead to the upper deck.

STABILITY
Metacentric height is given as 8.53ft, and they were accounted excellent sea-boats though the casemates were wet, and they were rather slow in turning. Tandem rudders were fitted.

MACHINERY
There were 14 double ended coal fired Navy type (Schulz-Thornycroft) boilers and 4 double ended oil fired working at 235lb/sq in and arranged in 12 boiler rooms, 6 on either side of a centreline bulkhead. The foremost 4 rooms each had 1 oil-fired boiler, the next 6 each 2 coal-fired and the 2 aftermost each 1 coal-fired. Some oilfuel sprays were later provided for the coal burning boilers. The usual 2 sets of Parsons turbines with an impulse ring in each HP, drove 4 shafts. The 2 forward engine rooms housed the HP turbines on the wing shafts and were located on either side of 'X' turret, with the turbo-dynamo rooms on the lower deck above, while the 2 after engine rooms between 'X' and 'Y' housed the LP turbines and the main condensers over them. Nominal designed shp was 63 000 = 26.5kts, legend fuel 985 tons (¼ oil) and full load 3640 tons coal and 985 tons oil. The astern turbines developed 28 000 shp. The radius of action was about 3100 sea miles at 24¼ kts and 5400 at 16kts.

The usual deep water mile at Neukrug in the Baltic was considered unsafe in wartime, and they were tried on the Belt mile in 115ft of water. Derfflinger was tried at 3¼ft over legend draught and attained 76 000 shp = 25.8kts at 271 rpm, while Lützow at about 1ft less draught reached 80 990 shp = 26.4kts at 277 rpm. These speeds were equivalent to 28.0 and 28.3kts respectively at legend draught in deep water.

GENERAL
In appearance they were fine well proportioned ships with straight stems and the usual pronounced rise of floor forward. Pole masts were originally provided but after Jutland Derfflinger had a heavy tripod foremast distinctive in that the legs were unusually wide apart. Lützow could be distinguished by a fully cased fore funnel, while Derfflinger's had a deep cap visible above the casings and was also slightly raised.

It may be noted that Derfflinger's designed main machinery weights totalled 2919 tons, of which boilers accounted for 1443 tons, turbines 1146, shafts 161 and propellers 35½. Auxiliary machinery weighed 566 tons plus another 10 if anti-rolling tanks were fitted. The coal-fired boilers with water to working level, but less other boiler room equipment, weighed 50 tons each and the oil-fired 68 tons each. Actual figures for Princess Royal which had the lightest machinery of the 13.5in battlecruisers, were: main machinery 4482 tons, of which boilers took 2327 tons, turbines 1803, shafts and screws 256. Auxiliary machinery weighed 491 tons. It is probable that these weights were not caculated identically in the two navies, but differences due to this were small. Comment is unnecessary.

Lützow was sunk at Jutland as described below and Derfflinger, scuttled at Scapa 21 June 1919, was raised for scrap in 1934.

WAR SERVICE
In the Dogger Bank battle on 24 January 1915 Derfflinger was third ship in the German line and smoke interference was worse than for the 2 leading ships so that it is not thought that she made more than 5 or 6 hits of the 22 — 11in or 12in recorded. She fired 234 — 12in APC and 76 base fused HE, engaging Lion, Tiger and Princess Royal, and also 86 — 5.9in and 5 — 3.45in mostly at the British light cruisers. Derfflinger was hit 3 times:

1   13.5in from Lion — burst very close to hull, shaking ship violently and causing some buckling and leaks.
2   13.5in from Princess Royal. Effect similar to No 1, but outer starboard shaft tunnel bent in addition.
3   13.5in from Tiger at 18 000yds. Burst on 12in belt at join between 2 plates which were forced in by up to 4in and 2in. Some flooding in wings and protective bunkers.

The damage was not serious and she was ready again on 17 February. There were no casualties.

At Jutland Derfflinger was second ship in the 1st Scouting Group and led them during the daylight hours after Lützow had dropped out. She expended 298 — 12in APC and 87 — 12in base fused HE and is estimated to have made 16 hits — 6 Princess Royal, probably 3 Queen Mary, 4 Barham, probably 3 Invincible. Other targets that can be identified were Lion, Valiant, Inflexible and the 2nd Light Cruiser Squadron. Derfflinger's greatest achievement was the destruction of Queen Mary in 11 salvos. She also fired 235 — 5.9in (117 base fused HE, 118 nose fused HE) at Princess Royal, Invincible and destroyers, and 1 torpedo at the British battleline which failed to hit.

Derfflinger was hit by 21 heavy shells, given in chronological order as follows:
'Run to South' None.
'Run to North'
1   15in from Barham or Valiant — holed skin plating 68ft forward of 'A' barbette and burst on main deck, which was torn up for about 16ft x 16ft and the upper main deck holed for a similar area. Much damage caused and fires started which could only be dealt with by using the foremost boiler room turbo-blowers to blow the smoke away forward. When steaming at high speed water entered and spread to compartments on the main and armour decks, about 1400 tons eventually entering the ship.

Derfflinger with tripod foremast
Drüppel

2 15in from *Barham* or *Valiant* — burst or broke up on skin plating 48ft from stern with unimportant damage inboard.
3 15in from *Barham* or *Valiant* at same time as No 2 — struck 10ft forward of No 2 and burst just inboard, tearing holes over 16ft diameter in main and quarter decks and causing much damage to light structures.
4/5 15in from *Barham* or *Valiant* struck together on the 4in port side armour and completely detached the 4th and 5th armour plates from the bows, covering an area of 17ft x 21ft. About 250 tons water entered the ship and a further 300 tons or so later.

First Fleet Action
6 12in from *Indomitable* — burst near hull in line with No 1 port 5.9in. Skin plating bulged below armour for about 40ft with gradual leakage in wings and a protective bunker.
7 12in APC from *Indomitable* — burst on 12in belt aft, at join between 2 plates which were forced in 1½in max.
8 12in APC from *Indomitable* at same time as No 7 — burst on side armour aft where 10¼in thick. Plate displaced by 1½in max. Torpedo net and net stowage damaged for 40 ft and part of net trailed in water above port outer propeller Engines had to be stopped for 2 minutes to secure net.

Second Fleet Action
9 15in APC from *Revenge* — struck 'Y' turret roof close below join between sloping and flat plates, and burst with relatively small effect on right cartridge hoist about 4ft from impact. A total of 7 main and 13 fore charges were ignited. In the gunhouse the 1in splinter bulkhead was not holed and 2 main and 2 fore charges at the left gun were not burnt. All but 1 of the turret crew of 75 were killed. Gas spreading through voice-pipes caused the starboard transmitting station to be abandoned for 8 minutes.
The next 8 hits occurred within at most 4 minutes:
10 15in APC from *Revenge* — pierced 10¼in 'X' barbette — the only instance in the war of a British shell piercing heavy German armour — and burst in upper part of turntable between the guns. A total of 7 main and 7 fore charges were ignited but in the gunhouse 1 main and 1 fore charge at the left gun did not ignite. Of the turret crew 6 managed to escape.
11 15in APC from *Revenge* — passed through fore funnel without exploding.
12 12in APC from *Colossus* — grazed 10¼in armour of 'A' deflected on to 1in upper deck and then overboard.
13 12in APC from *Colossus* — burst on 3in port shield of No 3 port 5.9in, completely wrecking the gun. Splinter damage in casemate and to No 4 gun.
14 12in APC from *Colossus* — struck 12in belt below No 6 port 5.9in and broke up or burst in holing armour. Some water entered the wings and an outer bunker.
15 12in APC from *Colossus* — struck and broke up in holing side armour aft where 10¼in thick. This hit

was on a join and pieces were broken off both plates, one fragment 11in x 10in travelling 30ft and piercing $2\frac{1}{4}$ft of plating.

16   12in APC from *Colossus* — ploughed a narrow furrow across the starboard side of the quarterdeck and burst, tearing a hole of about 10ft diameter. Considerable damage to cabins on main deck.

17   12in HE from *Collingwood* — hit superstructure side in line with bridge and burst in sickbay. Holes of about 18ft x $7\frac{1}{2}$ft in superstructure side, of about 15ft x 12ft in superstructure deck and of about 8ft x 8ft in deck above. 1in battery roof deck also holed for about 5ft x $2\frac{1}{4}$ft and much damage caused in vicinity of burst.

The next 3 hits also occurred within a few minutes of each other:

18   15in from *Royal Oak* — through after funnel without exploding.

19   15in from *Royal Oak* — through base of after funnel at boat deck level without exploding.

20   12in APC from *Bellerophon* — struck 12in CT armour obliquely and broke up or burst. A splinter destroyed the range-finder in 'B' turret, where the director-pointer had also failed.

Last Daylight Action

21   13.5in from *Lion* — struck $10\frac{1}{2}$in armour of 'A' barbette obliquely, glanced off and burst, holing 1in upper deck for $11\frac{1}{2}$ft x 4ft with smaller hole in upper main deck. Turret briefly jambed.

In addition to the above hits by heavy shells, *Derfflinger* was hit by 2 — 6in from the 3rd LCS and about 7 — 4in from destroyers. At the end of the battle *Derfflinger* was estimated to have 3350 tons of flood water in her with a draught of 37ft 11in forward and 27ft 8in aft, but 1020 tons of this were in 'X' and 'Y' magazines and shell rooms, flooded after hits No 9 and 10, and not pumped out to prevent too much trim by the head. Another 206 tons were in the starboard wings aft, counter-flooded to correct a 2° list to port. As contrasted with *Seydlitz*, no attempt was made to steam at high speed during the night. Casualties totalled 157 killed and 26 wounded. The *Derfflinger* was docked in the Wilhelmshaven floating dock for preliminary repairs, previous to it accomodating *Seydlitz*, and then in the Kiel floating dock after the battleship *König*, from 22 June to 15 July 1916. Her repairs in Kiel Dockyard were not however completed until 15 October.

At Jutland *Lützow* led the battlecruisers as Vice-Admiral Hipper's flag and her shooting was probably the best of any of the German ships. Unlike the rest she fired 4 forward and 4 after guns alternately, at least during the 'Run to the South', instead of 1 gun per turret, and used base fused HE initially instead of APC. Altogether she expended about 380 — 12in of which about 200 were base fused HE and the Rest APC, and is estimated to have made 19 hits: 13 *Lion*, 1 *Barham*, estimated 2 *Invincible*, estimated 3 *Defence* — sinking *Invincible* and probably *Defence*. Her identifiable targets also included *Princess Royal*. She fired about 400 — 5.9in mostly at destroyers, but *Lion* and the light cruiser *Falmouth* can also be identified. A 23.6in torpedo was fired at *Tiger* and another at *Defence* without success.

As *Lützow* was sunk there were none of the wonderfully detailed German hit reports, but a reconstructed diagram

gives 31 hits and there is a mention of 42. Such reconstructions often over-estimate the number of hits, and *Lützow* was certainly hit by a number of 4in from destroyers and 6in from *Falmouth* and *Yarmouth*. The 'Nordsee' tables give 24 hits by heavy shells, and as this number accounts for all known damage it is adopted here:

'Run to South'

1/2   13.5in from *Lion* — on forecastle forward of 'A' and together made large hole in upper deck which later allowed much water to enter and spread above the armour deck as *Lützow's* draught increased forward.

3   13.5in from *Princess Royal* — struck 1in upper deck between 'A' and 'B' and burst wrecking forward dressing station.

4   13.5in from *Princess Royal* — struck belt armour below lwl abaft mainmast. Apparently little damage but ship severely shaken.

'Run to North'

5   15in from *Barham* or *Valiant* — burst on belt below wl and damaged armour. Flooding in wings which spread and filled No 1 port 5.9in magazine.

6/7   15in from *Barham* or *Valiant* — hit superstructure deck between funnels and pierced 1in battery roof deck inboard of casemates. Large hole blown in superstructure deck, put main and reserve wireless out of action, and much damage caused.

8   15in from *Barham* or *Valiant* — apparently hit port edge of battery roof amidships and burst above 1.2in armour deck. Armour deck little damaged but smoke entered transmitting station which was also heavily shaken, and fire control temporarily interrupted.

9   13.5in from *Princess Royal* — apparently hit superstructure side below CT. Minor damage.

First Fleet Action

10   13.5in from *Lion* — apparently far forward above side armour.

11   13.5in from *Lion* — went through 1in battery roof deck and port forward armour door of space between casemates, bursting just aft of 'B' barbette. Serious fire amongst damage control material stowed there.

The next 8 hits were all 12in from *Invincible* and perhaps *Inflexible*, and occurred within 8 minutes:

12/13   2 shells below water burst in or near the broadside torpedo flat. Water very quickly spread to other compartments fore and aft through strained or damaged bulkheads, ventilation trunks and voice pipes.

14/15   Appear to have hit below water near Nos 12 and 13.

As a result of these hits at least 2000 tons of water quickly flooded in, and the draught forward increased by nearly 8ft, so that for a time speed had to be reduced to 3kts to lessen the pressure on the 1.2in after bulkhead of the torpedo flat which was leaking badly. Water still continued to spread aft of the torpedo flat, and neither of the forward main leak pumps could be used while the drainage system which should have allowed leakage water to reach the midships pumps, was apparently not functioning with full efficiency. The above damage put *Lützow* out of action.

16   Struck forecastle forward of 1 and 2 — large hole in upper deck allowing water to enter and spread above armour deck as draught increased.

1 *Lützow*

2 *Derfflinger* with pole foremast, 1913
  Drüppel

17 Pierced belt amidships near 6in lower edge and lodged unexploded in wings.

18 Struck side armour below No 3 or 4 port 5.9in and burst. Some armour driven in and jammed No 4 gun permanently.

19 Burst on net shelf below No 5 5.9in.

Second Fleet Action

5 hits by 13.5in from *Monarch* and *Orion* at about 18 500 yds in 3 minutes, the first 2 from port and the rest from starboard as *Lützow* turned.

20 Struck 'A' right gun just outside turret. Gun wrecked but shell deflected by 10¼in face armour and by port shield, and only small splinters entered.

21 Went through battery roof deck just aft of 'X' and burst on or below 1in upper deck. 1.2in armour deck also torn up without damage to ammunition spaces below.

22 Struck starboard side armour below 'B'. Flooding, including No 1 starboard 5.9in magazine.

23 Struck 8¼in right side of 'B' turret. No shell splinters entered but armour holed and fragments driven in. Right gun out of action, but left gun ready again

after about 30 minutes. A 12in fore charge caught fire but flash doors, an unusual fitting in German turrets, prevented a main charge immediately above from doing so, and also kept flame out of the working chamber.

24 Struck 6in casemate armour of No 4 starboard 5.9in and apparently burst, but gun not out of action.

Towards evening further troubles arose from 'A' and 'B' ammunition spaces flooding. This was thought to have occurred from leakage at an emergency exit of the broadside torpedo flat, and from local lack of water-tightness at the port torpedo bulkhead and side longitudinal bulkhead. It appears that 'A' magazines first began gradually to fill at about 2000 GMT. 'A' shell room was next affected and then 'B' magazines. There was already too much flooding in the vicinity for drainage to be successful, though it seems that the water was kept down in 'B' at least for a time. *Lützow's* draught forward was still increasing at 2130 and water entering above the armour deck would shortly become a very serious problem. Her speed at this time was 11kts soon reduced to 7, but at 0045 on 1 June her draught forward started to increase again and it was clear that she could not be kept afloat much longer. Nearly all compartments forward of the CT and below the armour deck were flooded, and most of the ship above this deck and forward of 'A' also, while water entering the foremost 5.9in casemates found its way below and eventually the ship's control room and foremost oil fired boiler rooms had to be vacated. A last attempt to go astern failed as *Lützow* could not be steered against the wind and rising sea, her forecastle was partly submerged and the propellers coming out of the water. The escorting destroyers *G40*, *G38*, *V45* and *G37* took off her crew and at 0145 *G38* was ordered to torpedo her. The first torpedo ran under her aft, the draught being much reduced here, but the second hit amidships and *Lützow* heeled over to starboard and disappeared in 2 minutes. The last figures from her damage control indicate that 4209 tons water were present below the armour deck and 4142 tons above, calculated to increase the draught forward by $28\frac{1}{2}$ft and reduce it aft by 15ft. This does not include water in the ship's control room and foremost boiler rooms, and much more was present when *Lützow* was scuttled as the waterline was then at the upper edge of 'B' barbette indicating an increase of about 40ft in forward draught. Casualites were 115 killed and 50 wounded.

„Derfflinger"
zerschossen nach der Seeschlacht.
31.5.1916.   (Volltreffer +)

Damage to *Derfflinger* after Jutland, marked by white crosses on
the photo, 31 May 1916

Derfflinger at Kiel
Drüppel

HINDENBURG

TABLE 16: **HINDENBURG PARTICULARS**

Dimensions: As *Derfflinger* except 697ft 2in (wl) 698ft 2in (oa).
Legend displacement: 26 513 tons.
Deep load: 31 000 at 30ft 5½in forward 31ft 4¼in aft.

	Builder	Laid down	Launched	Commissioned for trials
HINDENBURG	Imperial Dockyard, Wilhelmshaven.	30.6.1913	1.8.1915	10.5.1917 (completed 25.10.1917)

According to British Intelligence the delay in her completion was partly due to the removal of material for the repair of *Derfflinger* after Jutland.

DESIGN

This ship, the last German capital ship of the First World War period to be completed, was an improved *Derfflinger*. Most details were as in the 2 previous ships, and only the differences are noted below.

ARMAMENT

The armament was generally as in *Lützow*, but the 12in mountings were DrhLC/1913 with a 25½ft rangefinder in each turret instead of the previous 10ft. In all 4 turrets the shell rooms were below the magazines with the latter on the lower deck and the shell hoists were not broken at the working chamber, though the cartridge hoists were. It was possible however to load 'B' and 'X' shell hoists from depot rooms on the upper main and armour (main) deck respectively. Elevation was 16° and Petravic gear was fitted. As completed there were 4—3.45in Flak L/45 AA

guns mounted by the fore funnel and the outfit of 23.6in torpedos was increased to 16.

ARMOUR

The side armour tapered to 8¾in instead of to 9in at the upper deck, and forward of 'A' it was 4¾in to 54ft from the bows, ending in a 4¾in bulkhead, with 1.2in plating to the stem. The after belt was as in *Derfflinger* but ended about 24ft from the stern, *Hindenburg's* additional hull length being mainly from finer stern lines. The sloping front roof of the turrets was increased to 6in at about 30°, and the fore CT roof to 6-3.2in.

MACHINERY

The boiler rooms were rearranged, with the 2 foremost having 1 oil-fired boiler each, the next 4 each 2 coal-fired then 2 each with 1 oil-fired boiler, 2 each 2 coal-fired and 2 each 1 coal-fired. Nominal designed shp was increased to 72 000 = 27.5kts, and max oil fuel to 1180 tons. On trials on the Belt mile at about 2¼ft over legend draught she made 95 777 shp = 26.6kts at 290 rpm, equivalent to 28.5kts at legend displacement at Neukrug.

GENERAL

A tripod foremast with the legs less spread than in *Derfflinger* was fitted before completion and she also differed from *Derfflinger* in having shallower funnel caps. *Hindenburg* was never in action and was scuttled at Scapa on 21 June 1919. She was raised for scrap 22 July 1930 and was still of sufficient interest to be examined by the Naval Construction Department.

Compared with *Tiger*, *Hindenburg's* boiler rooms occupied 243 000 cu ft and a floor area of 9480 sq ft against 325 000 and 11 900, not unexpected figures in view of small tube boilers, but considering both ships had direct drive turbines, the main engine room differences are remarkable. In *Hindenburg* they occupied 104 000 cu ft and 5110 sq ft and in *Tiger* 237 000 and 6970. The largest single compartments in *Hindenburg* were the port and starboard after engine rooms of 36 000 cu ft each, while *Tiger's* port turbine room had a volume of 76 400. Admittedly *Tiger* had more powerful engines but though *Hindenburg's* figures would never have passed the Admiralty Engineer-in-Chief, it is impossible to avoid concluding that there was much wasted space in *Tiger*.

Of the legend displacement, in *Hindenburg* the hull accounted for 30.7%, armament including turret shields 13.2%, armour and protection 34.1% main and auxiliary machinery 13.7%, figures for *Tiger* being respectively 34.3%, 12.65%, 25.9%, 20.7% — the price paid for heavy high freeboard hulls and ponderous machinery is well shown.

Hindenburg at sea during gunnery exercises, 1918
Drüppel

MACKENSEN CLASS
MACKENSEN, ERSATZ FREYA, GRAF SPEE

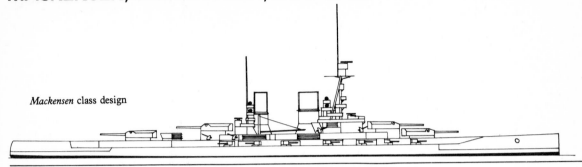

Mackensen class design

TABLE 17: MACKENSEN CLASS PARTICULARS

	Built	Laid down	Further History
ERSATZ VIKTORIA LUISE	Blohm & Voss	30.1.1915	Launched 21 April 1917 as *Mackensen*. Broken up 1923/4
ERSATZ FREYA	Blohm & Voss	1.5.1915	to have been named *Prinz Eitel Friedrich*. Launched to clear slip 13 March, 1920. Broken up 1920/22.
ERSATZ BLÜCHER	Schichau, Danzig	30.11.1915	Launched 15 September 1917 as *Graf Spee*. Broken up 1921/3.
ERSATZ A	Wilhelmshaven	3.11.1915	Later known as *Ersatz Friedrich Carl* to have been named *Fürst Bismark*. Broken up on slip 1922.
ERSATZ YORCK	Vulcan, Hamburg	.7.1916	Designed altered January 1917. Little ever done.
ERSATZ GNEISENAU	Krupp, Germania	Never laid down	Designed altered January 1917. Little ever done.
ERSATZ SCHARNHORST	Blohm & Voss	Never laid down	Designed altered January 1917. Little ever done.

Under the 1914-15 programme one ship the *Ersatz Viktoria Luise* was to be built and she was ordered from Blohm and Voss on 14 August 1914 together with a sister ship *Ersatz Freya* under the war estimates. A further 5 ships of the same class were ordered in April 1915, but none of the 7 were ever finished, though it was originally hoped to complete them from the summer of 1917 to the autumn of 1918.

As will be seen little progress was made due to labour shortages and the demands of the U-boat and destroyer programmes. In general layout the class resemled the *Hindenburg* but a full length forecastle deck was added and they were considerably larger with dimensions 731ft 8in (wl and oa) x 99ft 9in x 27ft 6½in mean for a legend displacement of about 30 500 tons.

ARMAMENT

Discussions over the main armament went on throughout 1913, 12in, 13.4in, 13.8in and 6—15in having their advocates, and in May 1914, 8—13.8in SKL/45 in 4 twin turrets arranged as in *Hindenburg*, were finally chosen. This gun fired a 1323lb shell at about 2700 fs and it may be noted that some of the outer forgings of these guns were eventually used for the long 8.3in that shelled Paris. The secondary armament of 12—5.9in SKL/45 in an upper deck battery was much less closely grouped than in the previous ships, extending from 'A' to 'X' and there were 8—3.45in Flak L/45. The torpedo tubes were increased to 5 submerged 23.6in (1 bow, 2 broadside forward of 'A', 2 broadside abaft 'Y') and no fewer than 27 torpedoes were to be carried.

ARMOUR

The main belt ran from 10ft forward of 'A' to 10ft past 'Y' and was 12in tapering to 6in at the lower edge and to 9½in at the upper deck and ending in 10-8in bulkheads. Forward and aft it did not reach the upper deck and was respectively 4¾in to about 68ft from the stem, continued with 1.2in plating, and 4in to about 36ft from the stern, ending in 4¾in (fore) and 4in (aft) bulkheads. The battery armour was 6in with 0.8in side and rear screens.

The barbettes were 11½in reduced to 4¾in (*Ersatz A* 6in) where behind the battery armour, and to 3⅛in behind the main belt and bulkheads, while the turrets had 12½in faces, 8in sides, 8⅛in rears, 7in sloping roofs and 4.3in flat roofs, except in *Graf Spee* where the faces were 12in, rears 8¼in, sloping roofs 6in and flat roofs 4in. Thr fore conning tower was 14-12in with 8in base and 6-4in roof and the after CT 8in with 3.2in roof.

The armour deck was at main deck level amidships and did not extend beyond the torpedo bulkhead so that there were here no deck slopes. It was 1.2in increased to 2.4in over ammunition spaces, while forward it was 2in at the belt lower edge and 3.2in to 4.3in aft a little above lwl at the crown. The upper deck was 1in over the main belt outside the battery area and the forecastle deck 2-1.2in over the 5.9in guns and 1in inboard. The torpedo bulkhead was 2in increased to 2.4in from 'A' to 'B' and 'X' to 'Y' and continued as a 1.2in splinter bulkhead to the upper deck.

MACHINERY

There were 32 boilers, 24 single ended coal fired and 8 double ended oil fired (smaller than in the previous ships). *Mackensen*, *Ersatz Freya*, *Graf Spee* and *Ersatz Scharnhorst* were to have had the usual 2 sets of Parsons type turbines with geared cruising turbines on the inner shafts, but *Ersatz A*, *Ersatz Yorck* and *Ersatz Gneisenau* would have had hydraulic transformers for the main turbines instead of direct drive, with geared cruising turbines on the outer shafts.

Nominal designed shp was 90 000 = 28kts, legend fuel 835 tons coal and 245 oil with deep load 3940 coal and 1970 oil. The number of leak pumps was increased from 5 in *Hindenburg* to 8.

GENERAL

They would have had a tripod foremast with 2 funnels and would have been fine looking ships. The rise of floor forward was much blunter than in *Hindenburg* and the 2 rudders were abreast instead of in tandem. Had the Germans hastened the construction of one or two of them, they might have had a devastating effect as no British battlecruisers likely to be completed by then, would have had much chance against them.

ERSATZ YORCK CLASS
ERSATZ YORCK, ERSATZ GNEISENAU, ERSATZ SCHARNHORST

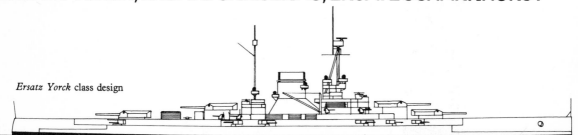

Ersatz Yorck class design

The new design for the last 3 ships of the previous class, *Ersatz Yorck*, *Ersatz Gneisenau*, *Ersatz Scharnhorst* was an attempt to produce a battlecruiser with 8—15in guns using the machinery already ordered. In April 1916 designs had been got out for ships of about 33 500-37 400 tons with this armament, but with 110 000—120 000 shp = 29-29.5kts and under 28kts had to be accepted if the 90 000 shp machinery were to be used. As previously stated only *Ersatz Yorck* was ever begun and her construction never got much beyond 1000 tons.

Compared with *Mackensen* length was increased to 747ft 5in (wl & oa) with the same beam and 28ft 6½in mean draught for a legend displacement of about 33 000 tons. The main armament of 8—15in SKL/45 guns, firing a 1653lb shell at 2625 fs (59°F charge temperature) or about 2655 fs (80°F) was arranged as in *Mackensen*, but the upper deck battery for the 12—5.9in SKL/45 was lengthened to 413ft with 6 guns from 'A' to the CT, 4 by the main mast and 2 by the after end of 'Y'. The 8 AA guns were to be either 3.45in or 4.1in Flak L/45 and the submerged TT were reduced to 3—23.6in with provision for the 27.5in J9 if ready. The bow tube was retained and the 2 broadside tubes were located aft of the boiler rooms, and thus within the area of the torpedo bulkhead. The ocutfit was 24 torpedoes.

The armouring was generally as in *Mackensen* but the main belt tapered to 8in at the upper deck forward, to 8½in amidships and to 9½in aft. Forward and aft the armour was now taken to the upper deck and stopped about 77ft from the bows. The battery armour was unchanged but the barbettes were 12in reduced to 7in behind the battery and to 3½in behind the main belt and bulkheads except that the fore part of 'A' was here 4½in. The turrets had 12in faces, 10in sides, 11½in rears, 10in sloping roofs and 6in flat roofs, and the fore CT roof was increased to 6¾-4in. The armour deck was reduced to 2.8-4in aft, and the forecastle deck to 0.8in inboard of the 5.9in guns, while the torpedo bulkhead was unchanged.

With 90 000 shp a speed of 27¼kts was expected, and boilers and engines remained unaltered, as did deep load fuel though legend was altered to 785 tons coal and 295 oil.

In appearance they would have been quite distinct with the uptakes trunked into one large funnel.

THE LAST GERMAN DESIGNS

TABLE 18: ARMOUR THICKNESSES FOR THE LAST GERMAN DESIGNS

DESIGN	4-16.5in	6-16.5in	8-16.5in
Main belt & Bulkheads (inches)	14 ($6\frac{1}{4}$ lower edge)	14 (10 upper edge, $6\frac{1}{4}$ lower edge)	12 ($8\frac{3}{4}$ upper edge, $6\frac{1}{4}$ lower edge)
Upper belt & bulkheads casemates*	8	$6\frac{1}{4}$	6
Barbettes	14	14	14
Barbettes behind upper belt	14	10	10
Barbettes behind main belt	10	6	6-4
Armour deck midships	3.2	2.4	2
Armour deck fore	2.8	2	2
Armour deck aft	$4\frac{3}{4}$	4	4
Torpedo bulkhead	2.8-2.4	2.8-2.4	2.4-2

* Upper belt is that part of side armour above main deck.

A number of sketch designs for battlecruisers were produced in late February-March 1918, though there was no prospect of them being built until Germany had won the war on land, an event which at times appeared quite probable in the spring of 1918. These designs differed in main armament — 4, 6 or 8 — 16.5in SKL/45, in armour and in speed but many features were common to all. There was a short forecastle reaching to the foremast or CT, and all had a middle deck above lwl so that the main deck was higher than in previous ships. Legend displacement was about 44 300 tons and dimensions 787ft (wl) x 110ft x 32ft 10in. The beam was limited by the 114ft 10in of the Wilhelmshaven locks, a small allowance being made for listing, but the length appears to have been determined by the allowable overhang in the Kiel and Wilhelmshaven floating docks, as the locks were 853ft long.

The secondary armament was 8—5.9in SKL/45 in casemates, 4 on the upper deck forward by the CT or fore turrets and 4 on the main deck near the after turret(s). There were also 4—5.9in Flak L/45 in single mountings, and 1—27.5in submerged bow TT only. There was no thin side armour at the ends, the main belt running from well forward of 'A' barbette to the rudder heads. In all designs the 16.5in twin turrets had 14in faces, 10in sides, 10in sloping front roofs and $6\frac{1}{4}$-6in flat roofs, the fore CT 14in with 10in base and the after CT 10in. The forecastle deck near the forward casemates and the upper deck were only 0.8in while the armour deck amidships at middle deck level was flat and did not cover the space between the torpedo bulkhead and the side.

There would have been 16 coal fired and 10 to 16 oil fired boilers, shp and speed figures being 180 000 = 31.5kts for the 4 gun, 160 000 = 31 for the 6 gun and about 135 000/140 000 = 30/30.5 for the 8 gun. The 6 gun design had 1 turret forward and 2 aft, and of this and the 8

gun there were 2 versions, one with the after turrets separated as in *Derfflinger* and the other with them as a close superfiring pair, the former version allowing 2 more boilers.

The 8 gun designs are shown with one large funnel and the others with two, and all with tubular fore and main masts. There was no rise of floor forward. The lessons of Jutland are clearly shown in the abolition of the broadside torpedo flats and in the heavy armour forward (and also aft), but the thin decks are to be noted though turret crowns were thickened. The hull form was not suited to high speeds, which had become important as German battleship designs now envisaged at least 26kts, and in May/June 1918 sketch designs for 2 lengthened 6—16.5in ships, which would have required new locks at Wilhelmshaven, were produced. These resembed the previous design with widely separated after turrets, armament and protection being unchanged, and the larger of the two would have been 886ft (wl) with the previous beam and a legend displacement of about 49 200 tons, 16 coal and 16 oil fired boilers and 220 000 shp for 32kts which seems pessimistic.

There were also some March 1918 designs inspired by the *Courageous* and *Glorious* which had been in action with German light cruisers in November 1917. The most remarkable of these was 787ft wl x $88\frac{1}{2}$ft x 27ft 3in with legend displacement of about 29 500 tons, 4—13.8in SKL/45, 4in side armour, 8in max on turrets and barbettes, and 48 boilers (8 coal, 40 oil fired) on 2 deck levels; 200 000 shp was expected to give 34kts.

Returning to the 16.5in ships, a comparison with the post 1918 British 'G3' design (previously described in *Warship*) will show that however well protected on and below the water line, the German designs were notably ill suited for long range actions when their thin decks would offer little protection.

RENOWN CLASS
RENOWN, REPULSE

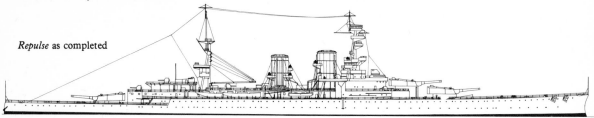

Repulse as completed

TABLE 19: **RENOWN CLASS PARTICULARS**

Dimensions: 750ft (pp) 789ft 9in (wl) 794ft (oa) x 90ft x 25ft (fore) 26ft (aft).
Legend displacement: 26 500 tons (*Repulse* actually 26 854 tons at 29ft 3in mean; *Renown* unknown).
Deepload: 30 835 tons at 29ft 3in mean (*Repulse* actually 31 448 tons at 29ft 9in forward, 29ft 7in aft).
Sinkage: 103 tons 1inch.
Freeboard: 32ft forward, 23ft 6in amidships, 19ft aft at legend draught.

	Builder & Machinery	Laid down	Launched	Completed	Joined Fleet
RENOWN	Fairfield	25.1.1915	4.3.1916	20.9.1916	28.11.1916
REPULSE	Clydebank	25.1.1915	8.1.1916	18.8.1916	21.9.1916

DESIGN

As shown above the development of German battlecruiser designs continued without interruption to 1918, but there was a break in British designs after *Tiger*. The 1912-13 programme contained 4 ships of the *Queen Elizabeth* class, nominally 25kt (actually 24kt) battleships, instead of the 3—21kt battleships and 1 battlecruiser originally envisaged (the 5th *Queen Elizabeth, Malaya,* was paid for by the Federated Malay States). Neither the 1913-14 nor the 1914-15 programmes included any battlecruisers, and of the 4 battleships of the latter programme, the 2 dockyard ships were cancelled and *Renown* and *Repulse,* contracted to Fairfield and Palmer's, suspended on the grounds that they could not be completed in time to take part in the war. After the Battle of the Falkland Islands, Lord Fisher who had returned as First Sea Lord, aided by the general battlecruiser euphoria, obtained sanction for *Renown* and *Repulse* to be redesigned as fast battlecruisers to complete in 15 months from laying down. As Palmer's had no slip long enough, the contract for *Repulse* was transferred to John Brown's at Clydebank. Work on the design began 19 December 1914 and it was formally approved 22 April 1915, but the builders had sufficient information to start work by 21 January.

ARMAMENT

The main armament of 6—15in/42 Mark I guns firing a 1920lb shell at 2472 fs was in 3 twin turrets with a superfiring pair forward and one aft. Gun axis heights were 35ft, 45ft and 23ft at designed legend draught.
The mountings were Mark I* in *Renown*, while *Repulse* had 2 Mark I* and 4 Mark I. These only differed in the method of transfer of shells from shell room to main trunk. Elevation was 20° and range 24 100yds. The magazines were above the shell rooms with their crowns at lower deck level, and the outfit was 120 rounds per gun, originally 60 APC and 60 CPC, then 72 APC, 24 CPC, 24HE and at the end of the war 84 APC (shellite filling) and 36 CPC. For the first time in battlecruisers there were 2 directors, one on the foremast and the other in an armoured hood on the CT roof.

Except that there were only 6 guns the main armament was very good, but **the secondary armament** of 17—4in/44.3 BL Mark IX was poor, particularly as 15 of the guns were in clumsy Mark I triple mountings, located to port and starboard on the forward superstructure, one forward of the mainmast, and two abaft it, superfiring over one another. The two remaining guns were in PXII mountings by the CT. It has had originally been intended to mount 4in/45 QF Mark Vs, but at that date these did not have the electric primers needed for director firing. The outfit was 150 rounds per gun (45 Common, 105 HE), later increased to 200 (50 CP, 120 HE, 30 HE Night Tracer). Directors for the 4in guns were located on the fore and main masts. There were 2—3in/20 cwt Mk I AA guns, each with 120 HE and 30 incendiary shells, and 2—3pdr Hotchkiss saluting guns. **The torpedo armament** consisted of 2 broadside submerged 21in TT forward of 'A' barbette and 10 topedoes were carried. It may be noted that *Renown* successfully fired a torpedo in 1916 while at full speed. In October 1917 a Sopwith Pup single-seater was for the first time flown off platforms on *Repulse's* 'B' and 'Y' turrets, and by the end of the war both ships had a Sopwith Camel on 'Y' platform and a '1½ Strutter' 2 seater on 'B'

ARMOUR

The armouring was scanty. The 6in main belt ran for 462ft between the centre lines of 'A' and 'Y', and was only 9ft wide, extending from the main deck to 1ft 6in below the

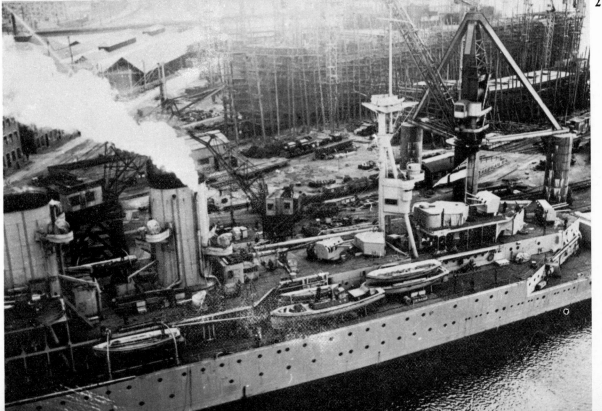

3

1 *Repulse* fitting out at Clydebank, 1916

2 *Repulse,* midships superstructure at John Brown's, 1916

3 *Repulse* as completed, 1916
Scottish Records Office

designed legend wl. It was continued at 4in forward and 3in aft, stopping well short of the ends. Above the belt the sides were 1½in plating with 1½-1in on the funnel uptakes between forecastle and shelter decks. The bulkheads were 4in at the ends of the 6in and 4in belt and 3in at the end of the 3in, the foremost bulkhead being continued to the upper deck, and the fore main belt bulkhead at 3in to the forecastle deck. The barbettes 30ft 6in internal diameter with 27ft roller paths, had only 7in armour reduced to 5-4in where behind bulkheads or belt ends, and the turrets 9in for the face and 2 front side plates, 7in for the 2 rear side plates and 11in for the rear plate, with 4¼in roof plates of better quality than in previous battlecruisers. The CT was 10in with 6 — 3in floor, 3in roof and 6-3in on the armoured director, and the after torpedo control tower 3-1in.

The armour deck at main deck level amidships was originally 1in flat with 2in slopes, but after Jutland and before completion, it was increased to 2in flat over the magazines. The forecastle deck was 1½-¾in between end barbettes. For the area of the belt ends main and lower decks were originally both ¾in, but the former was increased to 1¼in near 'A' and 'Y' before completion. Beyond the side armour the lower deck was 2½in.

The side was bulged out below the armour shelf, the double bottom curving round below the armour deck slope but in no sense were true 'bulges' fitted, nor was there any torpedo bulkhead though plans were made to increase the longitudinal bulkhead to 2-1½in at the price of 700 tons overweight but the 2 months delay in building was not accepted. Metacentric height was measured in *Repulse* at 3.45ft at legend displacement rising to 6.1ft at deep load.

MACHINERY
Although small tube boilers and lighter turbines would have been of great advantage, it was decided for reasons of time to use similar machinery to *Tiger's*. There were 6 boiler rooms extending over 193ft with 42 Babcock and Wilcox boilers (235lb/sq in), 3 in the foremost room, 7 in the next and 8 in the others. The 2 engine rooms and 2 condenser rooms occupied a length of 110ft and there were 2 sets of direct drive Brown-Curtis turbines. It is usually stated that the HP turbines were on the wing shafts and the LP on the inner, but contemporary turbine manuals state that when going ahead the steam first entered additional impulse turbines on the inner shafts before passing to the wing turbines. It was expected that 120 000 shp would give slightly under 32kts at legend draught (1000 tons oil fuel). Deep load stowage was 4243 tons oil for *Repulse* and 4289 for *Renown,* and the estimated radius of action about 3100 sea miles at 26½kts, and 4800 at 19.

On the Arran mile *Repulse* achieved 119 025 shp = 31.73kts at 275.1 rpm when displacing 29 900 tons at 28ft 2½in mean and *Renown* 126 300 = 32.58 at 281.6 rpm displacing 27 900 tons at 26ft fore, 27ft 3in aft. It can at least be said that whatever their faults the high designed speed could easily be met.

GENERAL
Their poor protection was looked on with much disfavour in the Grand Fleet, and on 20 October 1916 Admiral Jellicoe the C in C, proposed that additional protection be fitted. This was approved and the work done by the builders at Rosyth, *Repulse* being in hand from 10 November 1916 to 29 January 1917, and *Renown* from 1 February 1917 to 1 April 1917. The armour deck was increased to 3in on the flat and upper part of the slopes over the engine room, while the lower deck became 2in over the magazine crowns, 2½in forward of 'A' and abaft 'Y', and 3½in over the steering gear. The armour gratings were strengthened and 2in plating added to the lower CT bulkheads, the total increase in weight amounting to about 500 tons.

In appearance they were handsome ships particularly after the fore funnel was increased in height, with tripod fore and main masts, 'plough' bows and a pronounced sheer and flare forward.

The legend weights indicate the faults of the design (see table 20).

Respective 1917 deep load figures with max fuel were 32 633 and 32 074 tons, and later in the year *Renown* is given as 27 947/32 727 tons. Compared even with *Tiger* the lower armour and protection and the high hull weights (*Tiger* 25.9%, 34.3%) show the dubious features of the *Renown* design, and it may be noted that in spite of the hull's weight some weaknesses were revealed in service.

TABLE 20: RENOWN CLASS WEIGHTS

	Original Design	Repulse as completed	Renown 1917
Equipment (tons)	685 (2.6%)	685	685
Armament inc Turret shields	3335 (12.6%)	3420	3391
Machinery & Engineer's stores	5780 (21.8%)	6096	6155
Oil Fuel	1000 (3.8%)	1000	1000
Armour & Protection	4770 (18.0%)	15653	16189
Hull	10800 (40.7%)		
Board Margin	130 (0.5%)	Nil	Nil
TOTAL (tons)	26500	26854	27420
			(REPULSE 27333 tons)

Respective 1917 deep load figures with max fuel were 32 633 and 32 974 tons, and later in the year *Renown* is given as 27 947/32 727 tons. Compared even with *Tiger* the low armour and protection and the high hull weights (*Tiger* 25.9%, 34.3%) show the dubious features of the *Renown* design, and it may be noted that in spite of the hull's weight some weaknesses were revealed in service.

WAR SERVICE

Only *Repulse* was in action during the 1914-18 war, at the second Battle of Heligoland Bight on 17 November 1917 when she fired 54 — 15in CPC and scored 1 hit on the light cruiser *Königsberg* (the 2nd of that name), a raking shot which broke up in a bunker and temporarily reduced speed to 17kts.

Both ships had long careers during which thes were extensively reconstructed, and *Renown* served through the Second World War and was not sold for scrap until 19 March 1948 while *Repulse* was sunk by Japanese torpedo planes off Malaya, 10 December 1941.

View aft from the forecastle of *Repulse*
CPL

Renown, 1919
NMM

COURAGEOUS CLASS
COURAGEOUS, GLORIOUS

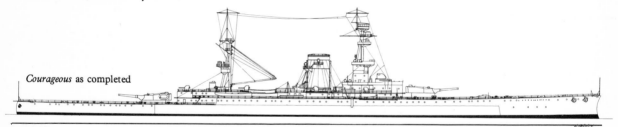

Courageous as completed

TABLE 21: **COURAGEOUS AND GLORIOUS PARTICULARS**

Dimensions: 735ft (pp) 786¼ft (oa) x 81ft x 21ft (fore) 22ft (aft).
Legend displacement: 17 400 tons (as originally designed).
Normal displacement: 19 320 tons at 23ft 3in (fore) and 23ft 5in (aft) — 1918 figures.
Deepload: 22 690 tons.
Sinkage: 89 tons/inch.
Freeboard: 28ft forward and 17ft aft at normal load.

	Built	Machinery	Laid down	Launched	Completed
COURAGEOUS	Armstrong, Walker	Parsons	28.3.1915	5.2.1916	.1.1917
GLORIOUS	Harland & Wolff, Belfast	Harland & Wolff	1.5.1915	20.4.1916	.1.1917

DESIGN

Authorisation for further battlecruisers could not be obtained in early 1915 and these ships, together with the *Furious*, were built as 'large light cruisers', though 'light battlecruisers' is perhaps a better description. They were intended originally for Fisher's Baltic Landing project, but it is difficult to see what role they could have played, except to lure German forces away for which their high speed and shallow draught would have been useful.

ARMAMENT

The main armament of 4 — 15in/42 Mark I guns was in fore and aft twin turrets, with Mark I* mountings giving 20° elevation. The outfit was 120 rounds per gun, comprising 72 APC 24 CPC, 24 HE but they had no HE in November 1917 and the immediate post war outfit is given as 36 lyddite filled APC and 84 CPC per gun. There were 2 directors as in *Renown*.

The secondary armament of 18 — 4in BLIX guns in 6 Mark I triple mountings was disposed on the shelter deck to port and starboard of the foremast and funnel and on the

1

centre line forward and aft of the mainmast. The original outfit was 150 HE per gun later increased to 250 (63 CP, 150 HE, 37 HE Night Tracer), and there were 2 directors as in *Renown*. 2 — 3in/20 cwt Mark I AA (160 HE each) and 2 — 3pdr Hotchkiss saluting guns completed the gun armament, and there were originally 2 submerged broadside 21in TT forward of 'A' with 10 torpedoes carried. 12 above water 21in TT in twin mountings were later added, and the total torpedo outfit increased to 20. As with *Renown*, *Glorious* successfully fired a submerged TT at full speed. *Courageous* was for a short period in the spring of 1917 fitted with mine laying rails aft to take 222 British Elia or 202 HII mines, but never laid any. By the end of the war both ships had a 'Camel' on 'Y' platform and a '1½ Strutter' on 'A'.

ARMOUR

The hull was protected on light cruiser lines with a maximum of 2in protective plate on 1in skin plating. The barbettes were 7in maximum and the turret shields as in *Renown*, while the CT originally 6in, was increased to 10in with 6-3in on the director hood. The forecastle deck was 1-¼in from 'A' barbette aft, and the upper deck 1in for some way forward of 'A' and also by 'Y'. The main deck was originally 1in on slopes and ¾in flat between barbettes, but after Jutland this was increased to 2-1¾in over magazines. The lower deck was 1in forward of 'A' and 1½-1in abaft 'Y', thickened to 3-2in over the rudder.

The hull was bulged out below the waterline but as in *Renown* there was no true bulge protection. 1½-1in torpedo bulkheads extending between barbettes were added during construction but these ran inboard of the wing engine rooms. Metacentric height was determined in *Courageous* as 3.85ft at legend and 5.8ft at deep load.

MACHINERY

For the first time in a large British warship, small tube boilers and geared main turbines were installed, the latter resembling a double installation for the light cruiser *Champion*. There were 18 Yarrow boilers (235lb/sq in) in 3 rooms with a single large funnel, and 4 engine rooms, each with a set of Parsons turbines geared to a propeller shaft. Each set comprised HP and LP ahead and astern turbines, the LP ahead and astern being in one casing. The outer shafts were driven from the wing engine rooms, the starboard inner shaft from the fore midships room and the port inner from the after midships room. Each engine room had a main condenser and there was also an auxiliary condenser in the wing rooms. The boiler rooms extended for 120ft and the engine rooms for 84ft, respectively 73ft and 26ft less than in *Renown*, but with less shp as the designed figures for the *Courageous* class were 90 000 = 32kts at 17 400 tons. Only *Glorious* was tried on the mile off Arran and achieved 88 550 shp = 31.25kts at 327.5 propeller rpm and 21 270 tons, so that 32kts was easily reached at normal displacement. Legend fuel was 750 tons oil and deep load 3250, the intended radius of action being 6000 sea miles at 20kts. Main and auxiliary machinery weights with engineer's stores, amounted to 2990 tons including the additional 610, compared with 5900 tons in *Tiger* and 3630 in *Hindenburg*, a great advance even over German figures, and showing the advantage of obtaining the necessary high turbine blade speeds by small diameter fast running turbines instead of the former large diameter ones.

GENERAL

The hull was heavy at 8500 tons designed weight, but on the night of 8 January 1917 *Courageous* was damaged while working up for a full power trial off May Island at 30kts

1 A post-war view of *Courageous*
By courtesy of John Roberts

2 *Glorious*, 1918
CPL

3 *Courageous'* forward turret and bridgework, 1919
NMM

with wind force 6-8. The forecastle deck between the breakwater and 'A' barbette was severely buckled, and the side plates between the upper and forecastle decks also buckled, while an oil fuel tank and a reserve feed tank were reported leaking. Additional stiffening (130 tons) was added to *Courageous,* and a year later to *Glorious* as a precaution.

They were handsome ships with the single large funnel and tripod fore and main masts, but of doubtful utility.

WAR SERVICE

Both were engaged in the second battle of Heligoland Bight on 17 November 1917 where one of *Glorious's* guns (left 'A') suffered splinter damage. *Courageous* expanded 92 — 15in CPC and *Glorious* 57, but only 1 hit was made, on the shield of one of the light cruiser *Pillau's* 5.9in guns with local damage. In addition the 2 ships fired 180 — 4in HE and 213 — 4in CP. The above performance of the 15in armament was far from satisfactory, but it may be noted that the British light cruisers only made 3 hits from 2519 — 6in shells.

Courageous was converted to an aircraft carrier in 1924-28 and *Glorious* in 1924-30, and both were lost, it might be said thrown away, in the Second World War when *Courageous* was torpedoed by *U29* on 17 September 1939 and *Glorious* sunk by the 11in guns of *Scharnhorst* and *Gneisenau* on 8 June 1940.

FURIOUS

DESIGN

The third of the 'large light cruisers' was an even more abnormal design, which was not carried through in its original form, as *Furious* was completed as part cruiser part aircraft carrier, and soon converted to the latter. She was laid down at Armstrong's Walker Yard 8 June 1915 and launched 15 August 1916, but on 19 March 1917 it was decided to abandon the original design, and she was completed with a forward flight deck and hangar 4 July 1917, Wallsend being responsible for the machinery. On 17 October 1917 the decision was taken to add an after flight deck and hangar which were fitted in December 1917-March 1918.

As originally designed *Furious* was 735ft (pp) 786½ft (oa) × 88ft × 20ft 6in fore, 21ft 6in aft, for a legend displacement of 19 100 tons, but as completed she was 19 513 tons at 19ft 8in fore, 24ft aft, with deep load 22 890 tons at 24ft 11in mean. Sinkage was 89 tons per inch, and as in *Courageous* the forecastle deck extended past the mainmast, but *Furious* was given 7ft more beam.

ARMAMENT

The armament was entirely different, the original design calling for 2 — 18in/40 Mark I guns in single turrets fore and aft, though the design allowed for 4 — 15in as in *Courageous* if the 18in proved unsatisfactory. The fore turret which had a designed gun axis height of 35ft was replaced by the forward flight deck and hangar but the after turret remained in the ship until the December 1917 alterations. This was on the upper deck but with a high barbette so that the designed gun axis height was 28ft 1in. Sighting hoods in the turret roof were abandoned for ports cut in the face. The roller path diameter was 27ft as in the twin 15in, but the rotating structure was angled out above, and the barbette internal diameter was 35ft 5in. The outfit was 120 rounds per gun (40 APC, 80 CPC) and there were 2 directors as in the previous ships.

The secondary armament of originally 8, as completed 11 — 5.5in/50 BL Mark I, a gun introduced into the Navy with the light cruisers *Birkenhead* and *Chester* taken over from Greece, was a great improvement over the 4in triples They were in PI* mountings, allowing 25° elevation, and

were disposed from just forward of the foremast to abaft the mainmast with 2 on the forward superstructure, 7 on the shelter deck and 2 on the forecastle deck. The outfit was 200 per gun (120 CPC, 64 HE, 16 HE Night Tracer). 2 — 3in/20 cwt Mark I AA guns (160 HE per gun) and 2 — 3pdr Hotchkiss saluting guns were carried, and there were 2 submerged broadside 21in TT forward of 'A' barbette with 10 torpedoes.

Aircraft. As completed the forward flight deck was 228ft × 50ft and the hangar could accommodate 10 planes, though initially 3 Short reconnaissance seaplanes launched from trolleys, and 5 Sopwith Pup single seaters were carried. It was just possible to land the latter on *Furious*, but the attempt was far more likely to end in disaster, and the Pups were to ditch in the sea and be picked up by the small carriers *Nairana* or *Pegasus* to avoid having to stop *Furious*.

ARMOUR AND MACHINERY

The armouring was generally as in *Courageous* but the turret shields were a uniform 9in KNC with 5in roofs, and the extra beam was taken up by shallow bulges. The machinery was also similar but the turbines were Brown Curtis which were heavier than Parsons, so that the machinery weights totalled 40 tons more at 3030 tons. Designed figures were 90 000 shp = 31.5kts, but *Furious* was not tried on the mile though 94 000 shp was attained at 329 propeller rpm corresponding to 2572 rpm for the HP turbines and 1376 for the LP. Oil fuel weights were 750 tons at legend and 3393 at deep load.

WAR SERVICE

Furious never fired her 18in gun in action, and after conversion to a full aircraft carrier it was found that eddies from the funnel and bridge made landing on the after flight deck hazardous, all but 3 attempts ending in crashes. She was reconstructed from June 1922 to September 1925, the funnel being replaced by smoke ducts discharging aft, and the foremast and bridges removed (the mainmast had been removed in the December 1917 alterations). In this guise she served through the Second World War and was not scrapped until 1948.

Furious with the 18inch gun aft
By courtesy of John Roberts

HOOD

TABLE 22: HOOD WEIGHTS

	AS COMPLETED	DIFFERENCE FROM 1917 LEGEND
Equipment (tons)	913 (2.2%)	+113
Armament including Turret shields	5302 (12.4%)	+47
Machinery and Engineer's stores	5969 (14.0%)	+669
Oil Fuel	1200 (2.8%)	—
Armour and Protection	13 650 (32.0%)	+100
Hull	15 636 (36.6%)	+686
Board Margin	—	−145
TOTAL (tons)	42 670	+1470

For the first time in a British battlecruiser the armour and protection figure reached a satisfactory level, and the fault was that it was not concentrated in heavy armour and a thick deck.

DESIGN

The origins of the *Hood* date back to a decision in November 1915 to construct an experimental battleship which was to be based on the armament, armour and shp of the *Queen Elizabeth,* but was to be of the least practicable draught and to incorporate the latest ideas in underwater protection. When the proposals were forwarded to Admiral Jellicoe for his appreciation, he maintained that there was no immediate need for new battleships, but a great need for new 30kt battlecruisers as the Germans were known to be building the *Mackensen* class.

Two specifications completed 1 February 1916 were for a ship with 8 — 15in, 12 — 5.5in, 8in belt, 9in barbettes and 120 000 shp, *No 1* with large tube boilers being 835ft (pp) 885ft (oa) × 104ft × 26ft = 39 000 tons and *No 2* with small tube, 790ft (pp), 840ft (oa) × 104ft × 25ft = 35 500 tons. Respective speeds were 30 and 30.5kts.

Four further specifications were completed 17 February 1916, all with small tube boilers viz:
No 3: 810ft (pp) 860ft (oa) × 104ft × 26ft = 36 500 tons, 8 — 15in, 160 000 shp = 32kts.
No 4: 710ft (pp) 757ft (oa) × 104ft × 25ft = 32 500 tons, 4 — 18in, 120 000 shp = 30kts.
No 5: 780ft (pp) 830ft (oa) × 104ft × 25ft = 35 500 tons, 6 — 18in, 120 000 shp = 30.5kts.
No 6: 830ft (pp) 880ft (oa) × 104ft × 26ft = 39 500 tons, 8 — 18in, 120 000 shp = 30kts.
All were to have 12 — 5.5in, 2 TT, 8in belt and 9in barbettes.

In March 1916 the Board examined these specifications and selected *No 3* to be worked out in detail. At the time this was the logical choice though with the advantage of hindsight a combination of *Nos 3* and *5* to give 6 — 18in guns would have been preferable. Two alternative versions of *No 3*, one with 12 — 5.5in and 4 TT, and the other with 16 — 5.5in and 2 TT were worked out and the legend and sketch designs submitted on 27 March 1916. The design with 16 — 5.5in was preferred, and approved 7 April 1916 when orders were placed for 3 ships: *Hood* (Brown), *Howe* (Cammell Laird) and *Rodney* (Fairfield), the 4th ship

Anson being ordered from Armstrongs in July 1916. Legend displacement of this design was 36 300 tons, with dimensions 810ft (pp) 860ft (oa) × 104ft × 25ft fore, 26ft aft and freeboard 32ft forward, 23ft 6in amidships, and 19ft aft, the forecastle deck extending to just forward of 'X' barbette. Deep load mean draught was 29ft. There were 8 — 15in/42 Mk I guns in 4 twin turrets allowing 20° elevation, 16 — 5.5in, 2 — 3in AA and 2 submerged 21in TT. The belt was 8in amidships with 5in and 3in above and 5in and 4in forward and aft, while bulkheads were 4in or 3in, barbettes 9in maximum, turrets 11-10in with 4½in roofs, the CT 10in and the TCT 6in. There was 1½in plating on the funnel uptakes, the forecastle deck was 1½in-1in, the upper deck 1in aft, the main deck 1½in, and the lower deck 2-1in forward and 2½-1in aft. Bulges with a 1½in torpedo bulkhead provided the underwater protection. Small tube boilers and geared turbines would provide 144 000 shp = 32kts and oil fuel was 1200 tons legend and 4000 at deep load.

In this design the hull accounted for 38.8% of the legend displacement, armour and protection for 27.8%, armament for 13.2% and machinery for 14.3%, not encouraging figures except for the low machinery weight.

Hood was laid down 31 May 1916, the date of Jutland, and after the loss of 3 battlecruisers in this action, work was suspended while investigations took place. As a result a modified design was approved on 4 August 1916, with a legend displacement of 37 500 tons at 9in deeper draught and a loss of perhaps ½kt. The 8in belt was made 1ft 8in wider and the 5in upper belt reduced to 3in, the turret faces increased to 15in and the roofs to 5in, and the forecastle and main decks increased to 2in maximum, while a few other minor improvements were made, and the number of dynamos increased from 4 to 8.

Further modifications were submitted by DNC in August 1916 involving a legend displacement of 40 600 tons with draught of 27ft 9in fore, 28ft 9in aft and 31kts speed. The belt was to be 12in, with 6in upper belt, 7-6in forward and 6in aft. The bulkheads were increased to 6-4½in the barbettes to 12in maximum and the turret sides and CT to 12in also. The elevation of the 15in guns was increased to 30°. Before this design was approved proposals for mounting 4 triple 15in turrets were requested, and sketch designs were submitted with 4 triple, 2 triple and 2 twin, and 3 triple 15in turrets all on the same length and maximum beam as in the 8 gun design and with similar protection, but with displacement increased to 43 100-40 900 tons and speed reduced to 30.5-30.75kts. The 8 gun design was approved and *Hood* was laid down for the second time on 1 September 1916 by John Brown's at Clydebank, who were also responsible for the machinery. She was launched 22 August 1918 and completed 15 May 1920. The 3 other ships of the class were laid down as follows: *Rodney* 9 October 1916 (Fairfield); *Howe* 16 October 1916 (Cammell Laird); *Anson* 9 November 1916 (Armstrong) — but they were suspended 9 March 1917 and finally cancelled in February 1919.

Even now *Hood's* design was not settled and as will be seen in the description of the ship, many alterations were made to the 40 600 ton design. The final legend of August 1917 had the original length and maximum beam but draught was 28ft fore, 29ft aft at 41 200 tons and as completed she was 42 670 tons with dimensions 810ft 5in (pp), 850ft 7in (wl), 860ft 7in (oa) × 104ft 2in × 27ft 11in (fore), 30ft 7in (aft). Deep load was 46 680 tons at 32ft mean and sinkage 126.8 tons/inch. The forecastle deck extended to well abaft the mainmast, and there was a pronounced sheer and flare to the hull side with 'clipper' bows. Freeboard as completed was 29ft forward, 21ft midships and 17ft aft. The bending moments in the hull were large and the midships skin plating 1½-2in thick.

ARMAMENT
The main armament of 8 — 15in/42 Mark I guns was in superfiring pairs of twin mountings located forward and aft, with gun axis heights at load draught as completed: 32ft, 42ft, 30½ft, 20½ft. The mountings were Mark II allowing 30° elevation with loading at any angle up to 20°, with compressed air run-out and flash doors in the gun loading hoist well and elsewhere, which were not originally fitted in the Mark I mounting. As in *Furious* there were no sight hoods in the turret roofs, ports being cut in the face. The compressed air run-out allowed full salvos without overloading the hydraulic system and the 30° elevation gave a range with 4 crh shells of 29 850yds. A 30ft range-finder was fitted in each turret and there was also one on the armoured director tower, while the other director at the fore top had a 15ft range-finder. The magazines were above the shell rooms in *Hood* and the outfit of 120 rounds per gun comprised 84 shellite filled APC and 36 CPC.

The secondary armament of 16 — 5.5in BL Mark I guns in CP II mountings giving 30° elevation, was in open back 1½-1in shields with 12 guns on the forecastle deck and 4 on the shelter deck located from the foremast to abaft the mainmast, but to save weight for extra horizontal protection, the 2 aftermost guns on each deck were removed before completion. There were port and starboard directors for the 5.5in, and 150 rounds per gun were carried (38 shellite filled CPC, 90 HE, 22 HE Night Tracer). The guns were supplied by dredger hoists from ammunition passages which were themselves fed by other dredger hoists from the 5.5in magazines and shell rooms.

The upper dredger hoists were fitted as a result of the *Vengeance* flash trials in August 1917-January 1918 and would accommodate charges in Clarkson's cases.

There were 4 — 4in/45 QF Mark V AA guns in Mark III HA mountings allowing 80° elevation, located abaft the mainmast on the forecastle deck with 160 HE and 40 incendiary shells per gun, and 4 — 3pdr Hotchkiss saluting guns. The torpedo armament was to have comprised 2 submerged and 8 above water broadside fixed tubes on the upper deck, but 4 of the latter were removed in July 1919 to save weight for extra deck protection which was never fitted. Three 15ft range-finders were provided for the torpedo armament. Aircraft flying off platforms were carried for a time on 'B' and 'X' turrets.

ARMOUR
The side armour was inclined at 12° maximum to increase the angle of impact of enemy shells. There was 562ft of 12in between end barbettes extending from 4ft below to 5ft 6in above lwl as completed, and this was continued for some distance fore and aft at 6-5in and 6 in respectively. There was also a 3ft wide strip of 3in armour below the main belt abreast the boiler rooms. The original 6in upper belt was altered to 7ft of 7in armour between end barbettes, continued forward at 5in as far as the 6in side below, and to 9ft of 5in armour reaching to the forecastle deck and extending from 'A' barbette to abaft the main mast. There were 4in bulkheads at 'A' and 'Y' barbettes, and 5in at the ends of the side armour.

The barbettes had the same internal and roller path diameters as in previous 15in ships and were a uniform 12in above decks but differed below. 'A' was 10-6in between forecastle and upper decks (10in on forward face), 5in to the main deck and the forward part 2½in to the lower deck. 'B' was 6in to the upper deck and 5in to the main deck, and 'X' 6in to the main deck. 'Y' was continued at 12in to some way below the upper deck, and was 9-6in at the main deck and 5-2in at the lower deck, the greater thicknesses being on the after face. Except where noted, the barbettes had only ½in trunks between main and lower decks. The turrets had 15in faces stepped into a heavy 17in glacis plate of unhardened armour, 12in front side plates and 11in rear sides and rears, with 5in roofs. 2-1in protective plating was provided for the 5.5in working spaces and 1in for the ammunition passages, but 'box' protection for the above water torpedo warheads was removed in July 1919, and the tubes were no longer considered as war fittings, though they and their torpedoes were still carried when *Hood* was blown up.

The conning tower was very large and was 11-9in reduced to 9-7in on the lower part, with a 6in base thinned to 3-2in between decks. The roof was 5in and the director tower on it 6-2in. The after torpedo CT was reduced from 6in to 1½in in the July 1919 alterations, but retained its 3in roof.

The deck protection was much increased during construction. The forecastle deck remained at 1½in by the forward barbettes and was 1½-1½in, locally 2in over the boiler and engine rooms and ¾in at the after end of the deck. The upper deck was increased from 1in to 2in over the forward 5in upper side armour shortly after laying down, and also from 1in to 2in over the after magazines,

Hood dressed overall, June 1931
CPL

ɪᴇmaining at 1-¼in amidships and to the stern. The principal armour deck was at main deck level and over the boiler and engine rooms it was 2in on the outer part of the flat deck and 1½in over most of the area, while over the magazines it was increased from 2in to 3in in September 1916. The deck slope to lower deck level was 2in, and in May 1919 the 3in flat deck over the magazines was extended to the side of the hull above the slope. Forward the main deck was 1in over the 5in waterline armour and it was 2in over the 6in after belt. The lower deck was 1in at the stem, 1½in forward of 'A' barbette, 1½in aft of 'Y' (increased from 1in September 1916) and then 1in with 3in over the steering gear. Where forming the magazine crowns the lower deck was originally 1in, increased to 2in in August 1918 but not to the hull side. As a result of firing trials it was decided in July 1919 to increase the main deck to 5in over the forward and to 6in over the after magazines, but this was never done though the torpedo equipment and its protection were reduced as noted above to accommodate the additional weights.

There were bulges for 562ft amidships of 11ft maximum width. The outer section consisted of water tight compartments with 5 rows of crushing tubes inboard. Next came a 1½in bulkhead formed in way of the boiler and engine rooms by the true hull side continued downwards at 11° inclination. By the barbettes the hull side ran between the outer water tight compartments and the crushing tubes, and was not specially thickened, and here the 1½in bulkhead was a separate structure. By the barbettes and the boiler rooms there were next oil fuel tanks or other compartments with a ¾in bulkhead inboard and with a small air space between this and the boiler rooms. By 'A' and 'Y' handing rooms the ¾in bulkhead was increased to 1¼in, and the transverse bulkheads at 'A' and 'Y' were 1½in except between the lines of the longitudinal bulkheads when they were ¾in. There was not sufficient space for the inner part of this system by the engine rooms, and the forward engine room was directly inboard of the 1½in bulkhead, though there was space for a line of water tight compartments between this and the middle and after engine rooms. As some additional protection for the engine rooms, the outer boundary of the crushing tube space was increased from ½in to ¾in over their length.

Designed metacentric height was 4.15ft at legend and 4.9ft at deep load, and actual figures as completed were 3.25ft and 4.2ft which were quite inadequate for a ship of *Hood's* importance though tending to make her a steady gun platform.

MACHINERY

The boiler and engine rooms occupied nearly as great a length as in *Renown* but the total designed machinery weights were 480 tons less and SHP at least 24 000 more. There were 24 Yarrow small tube boilers (235lb/sq in) in 4 rooms, and 4 sets of Brown-Curtis geared turbines each driving a single shaft though some of the class would have had Parsons turbines. Each set comprised a high pressure and a low pressure ahead turbine with an astern turbine in the LP casing, and the wing shafts also had cruising turbines, clutched out at full power. There were 3 engine rooms with the turbines for both wing shafts in the forward one, those for the port inner shaft in the middle room, and for the starboard inner in the after room. The pitch circle diameters of the HP and LP turbines were 4ft 9in and 8ft 8in to 9ft 1in respectively compared with 10ft 6in and 11ft 0in in *Renown*. Designed full speed propeller rpm were 210 corresponding to 1497 for the HP and 1098 for the LP turbines, and designed shp 144 000= 31kts. Legend fuel was 1200 tons oil and normal deep load 3895 giving a radius of action of 7500 nautical miles at 14kts.

On the Arran mile *Hood* attained 151 280 shp = 32.07kts at 207rpm and 42 200 tons, while at 44 600 tons the figures were 150 220 shp = 31.89kts at 204 rpm. These were highly satisfactory figures, but more subdivision of the machinery spaces, and a reduction in the area occupied, would have been desirable from the point of view of fighting power.

GENERAL

In appearance *Hood* was a uniquely beautiful and powerful looking ship, the only fault to the writer's mind being the unusually noticeable rise in the quarter deck abaft 'X' and 'Y'

The 3 cancelled ships would have differed in important ways and would have formed a separate class. Trials in the Chatham float had shown that if a mine exploded under a magazine, it was preferable to have the latter below the shell room, as the water would flood in more quickly and had a better chance of preventing a magazine explosion, and as the lower position gave less chance of a shell reaching the magazine, it was decided in August 1918 to exchange the magazine and shell room locations in the 3 suspended ships. This involved reducing the outfit to 110 rounds per gun in 'A' and 'B' and to 100 in 'X' and 'Y' while the hull would have been filled out to accomodate 'Y' handing room with a slight loss in speed. The turret crowns would have been 6in, as intended for *Hood* but the 5in plates had been rolled, and the armour altered in other ways but it is clear now that further tinkering with the *Hood* design would not have produced a satisfactory ship.

The *Hood* was blown up on 24 May 1941 by the *Bismarck*.

CONCLUSIONS

Returning to the battlecruisers' heyday in the 1914-18 War, there is no doubt that the German vessels were better fighting ships due to weight savings in hull and machinery, but also because the propellant charges for their guns did not explode if an ammunition fire occured. The main defect shown in action was flooding forward which ultimately led to the loss of the *Lützow* and the near loss of the *Seydlitz*, though the former would have kept afloat if her water tight integrity had been of the usual German standard, and the latter's condition would have been far better if she had kept to a reasonable speed during the night of 31 May/1 June 1916. Amidships, German underwater protection was very good for the period and far better than in any completed British battlecruisers.

The faults of even the better protected British battlecruisers were well displayed by the damage to *Lion* at the Dogger Bank battle, but a still worse defect was the extreme violence with which their propellant charges ignited in the event of a fire in turret or barbette. This was well shown in *Lion* at Jutland and was responsible for the loss of *Queen Mary, Invincible* and in all probability *Indefatigable*. The British charges with a 16oz fine grain black powder igniter on each heavy gun quarter charge, needed very complete flash precautions — not fitted till after Jutland — to be safe in action, while the German charges with an igniter well protected by the brass case of the main charge, and a fore charge with no igniter, would not blow up the ship even in the case of a fire like that in *Seydlitz* at Dogger Bank. German flash precautions were sketchy as is well shown in all battlecruiser 11in and 12in turrets where the cartridge hoists entered the gunhouse near the cradle trunnions and the charges slid down open slides to the loading trays.

Other faults in British battlecruisers were the poor performance of their APC shells, largely due to the use of lyddite as a burster, and their indifferent, and at times downright bad, shooting. If they had shot as well as the battleships *Barham, Valiant* and *Iron Duke* did at Jutland, and had had reasonably good APC shells and flash precautions matched to the British charges, a much fairer comparison of the actual ship designs' behaviour in action could have been made: but none of this would have changed the failure of *Lion's* protection against 11in and 12in shells at the Dogger Bank.

Seydlitz scuttled at Scapa, 1918
Drüppel

now subscribe to **Warship** quarterly

A high quality journal, **WARSHIP** is devoted to the design, development and service history of combat ships. The scope is truly international, unlimited by period, nationality or ship type, although the emphasis is on the major navies of the present century.

Detailed and accurate information is the keynote in all articles — fully supported by plans, tables and photographs — and it is the aim of **WARSHIP** to encourage an original approach to popular subjects as well as to cover the unusual and little-known aspects of warship history.

In the same format as this '*Special*' — 72 pages, $9\frac{1}{2}''$ x $7\frac{1}{4}''$

Some articles from 1978 include:
The battle of Tsu-shima, the first Austrian submarines, *Essex* class carriers, the origins of the magnetic mine, a 7-turret *Colony* class cruiser design, US 'Treaty' cruisers, Type 15 and Type 16 fast frigate conversions, *Viribus Unitis* class battleships, cruiser radar, USS *California*, the Italian *Capitani Romani* class, the war service of Japanese B type submarines, *Leander* class conversions, the US 5inch 38 cal DP gun, Iranian *Saam* class destroyers, and Soviet G-5 type MTBs.

The four issues for 1977 are still available, individually at £2.00 per copy (+ 25p postage), or as a single hardback volume **WARSHIP VOLUME I** at £9.50 (+ 50p postage).

Available from specialist booksellers or direct from the publishers, **Conway Maritime Press Ltd, 2 Nelson Road, Greenwich, London SE10 9JB, UK.**

Annual subscription for 4 issues including postage £9.00 (UK) £12 (overseas). Specific rates on application. Free illustrated brochure available on request.

BELOW: *A Soviet G-5 MTB (series 11) fitted with shore bombardment rocket launchers. From Przemyslaw Budzbon's article in Warship 8.*

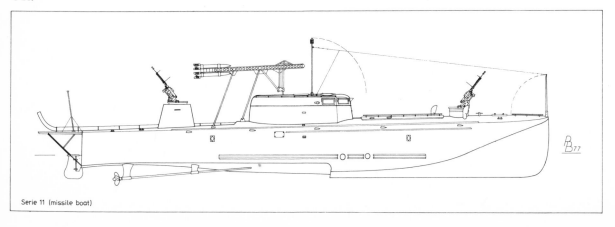

Serie 11 (missile boat)

WARSHIP SPECIALS are a new series devoted to technical and historical aspects of warships.

The 72 page format is the most detailed and flexible 'monograph' approach ever devised for this subject, each title containing up to 35 000 words, 70 photos and as many plans and diagrams.

For both the in-depth information and illustrations essential to modelmakers, wargamers and naval enthusiasts, WARSHIP SPECIALS are second-to-none.

Also in this series:

No 2
SUPER DESTROYERS
edited by
Antony Preston

£2.50

BATTLE CRUISERS

"There's something wrong with our bloody ships today!"

Beatty's indictment of his battlecruisers at Jutland is well-known, and the German side of the story is equally familiar — *Lützow* sinking after suffering tremendous damage; *Derfflinger, Seydlitz* and their consorts limping home in a shattered state. But were the British ships as bad as historians have claimed — or the German ships as good?

In this new study N J M Campbell challenges the accepted view and reinterprets the British and German designs in the light of their battle-experience. The origins of the battlecruiser type, wartime developments, and even the later projected designs are all covered in detail, telling for the first time the full story of the ships which formed the spearheads of both the German High Seas Fleet and the British Grand Fleet.

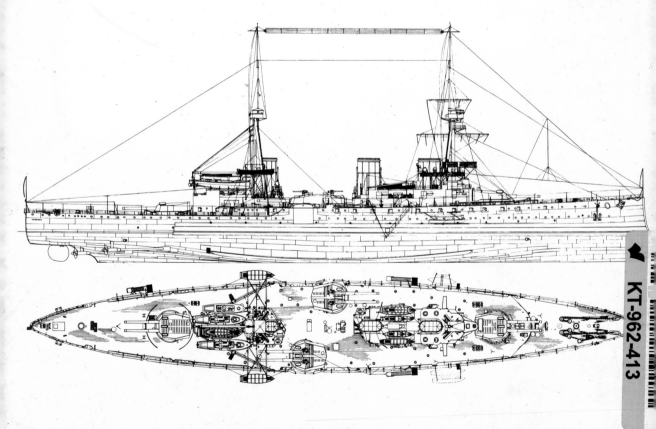

CONWAY MARITIME PRESS GREENWICH

£2.50 net ISBN 0 85177 130 0